(SEHR LANGSAM)

LIEVEN LEFERE

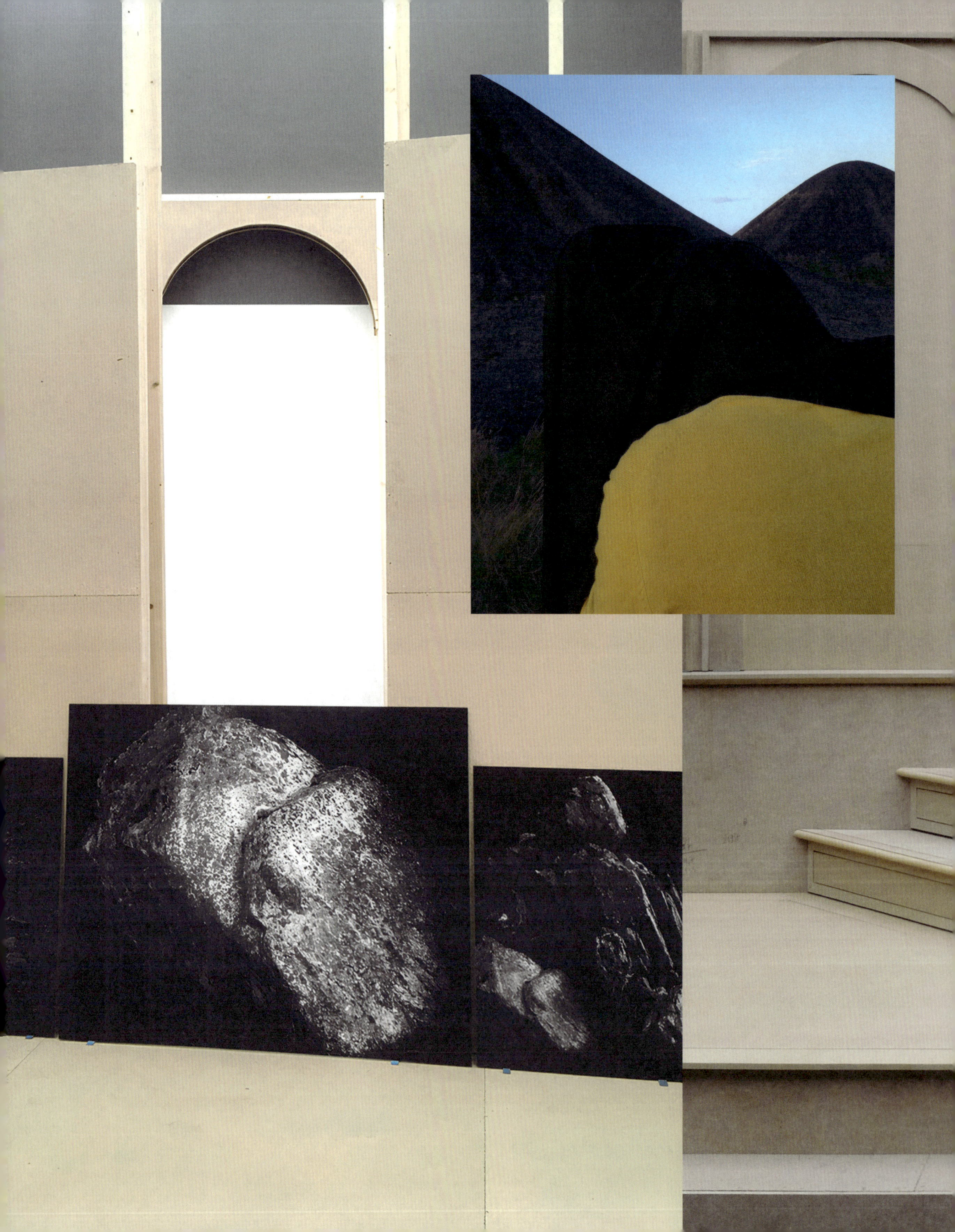

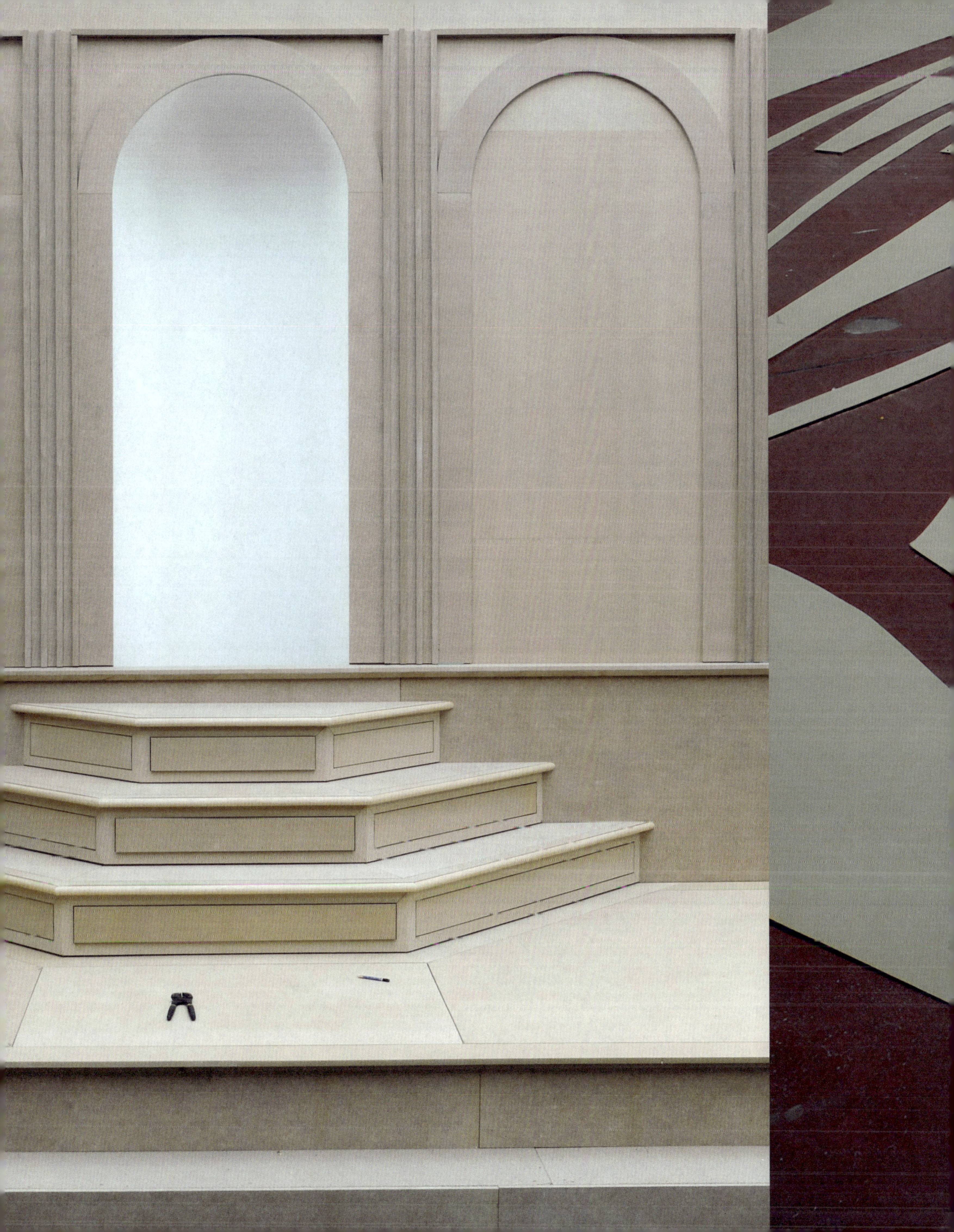

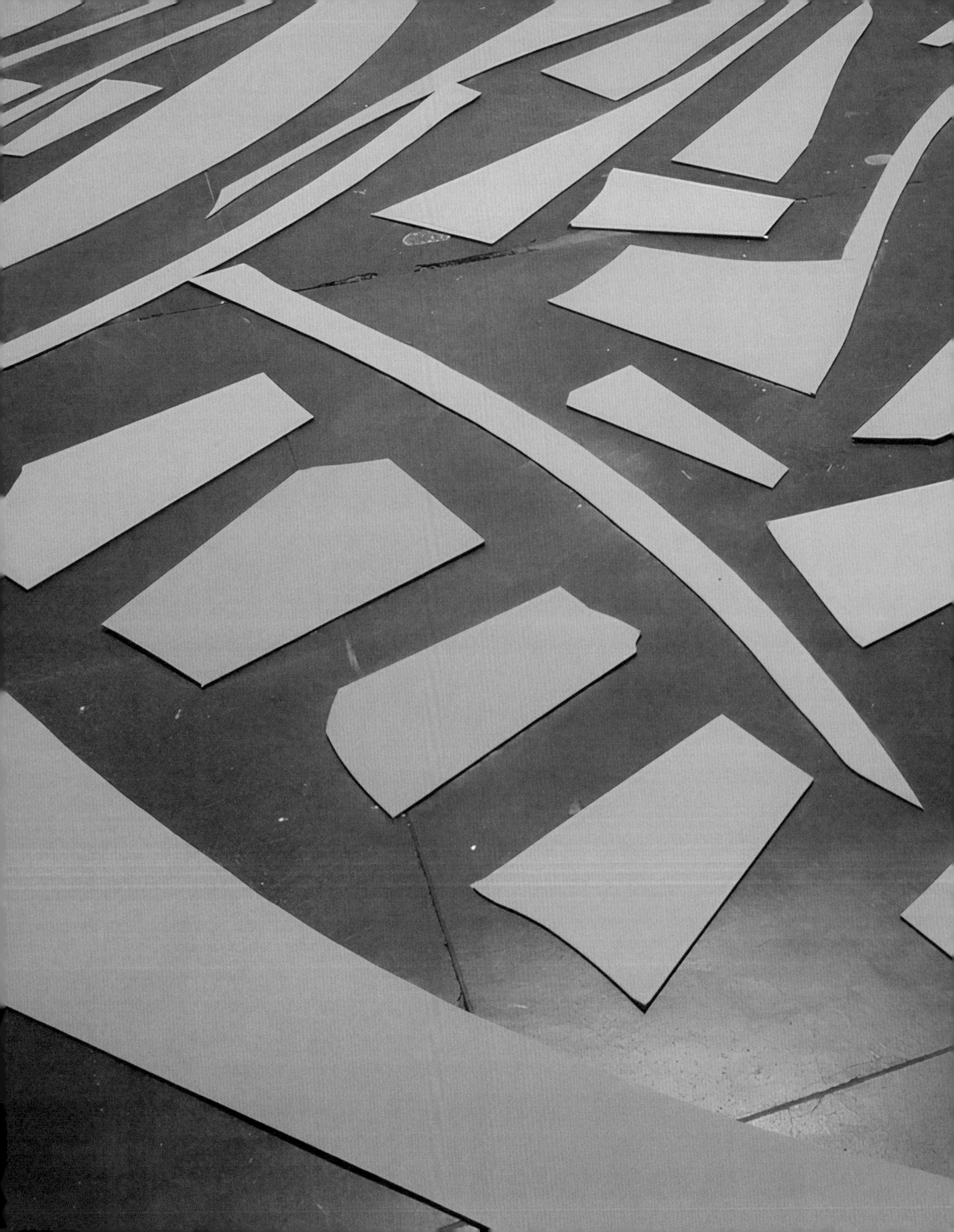

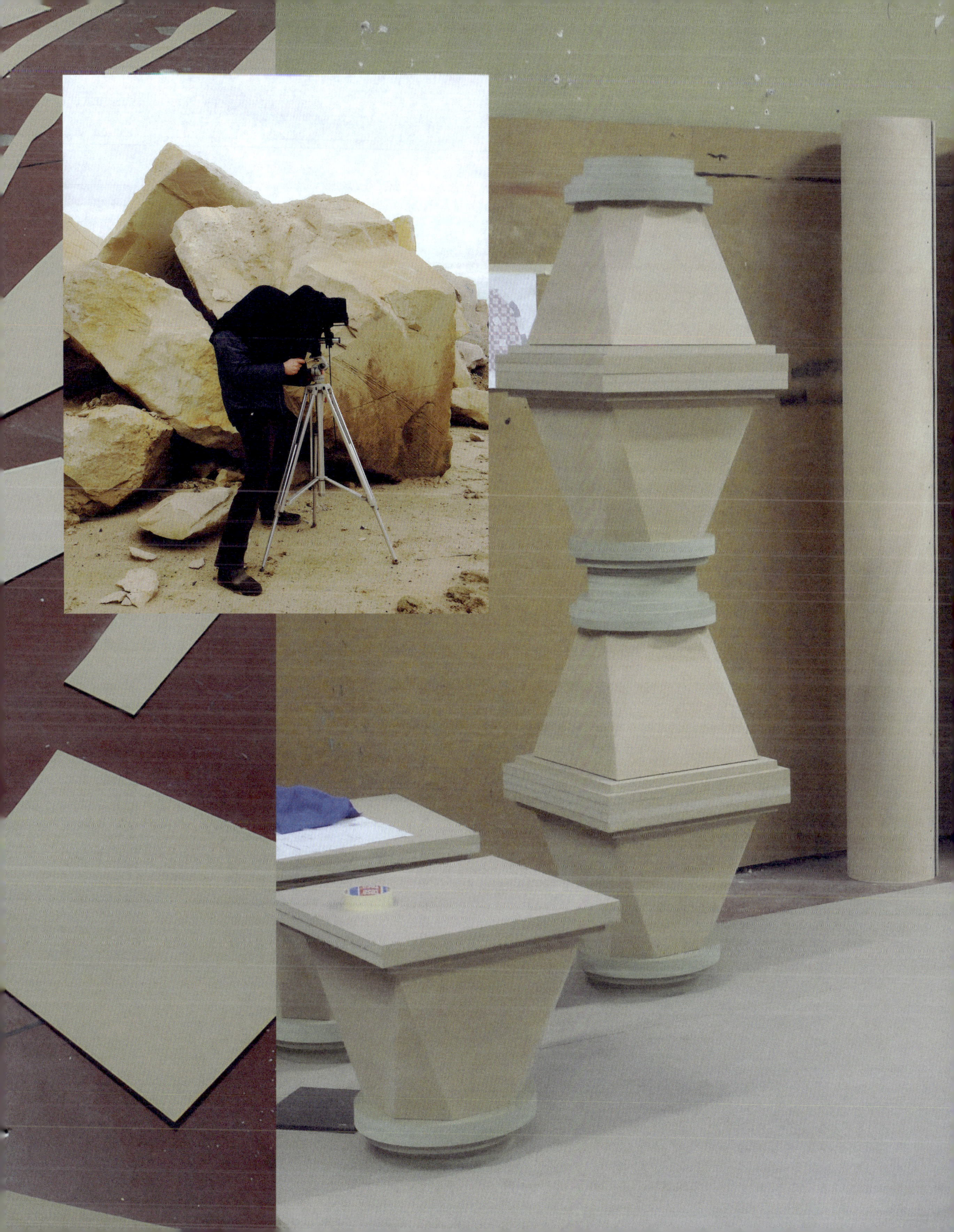

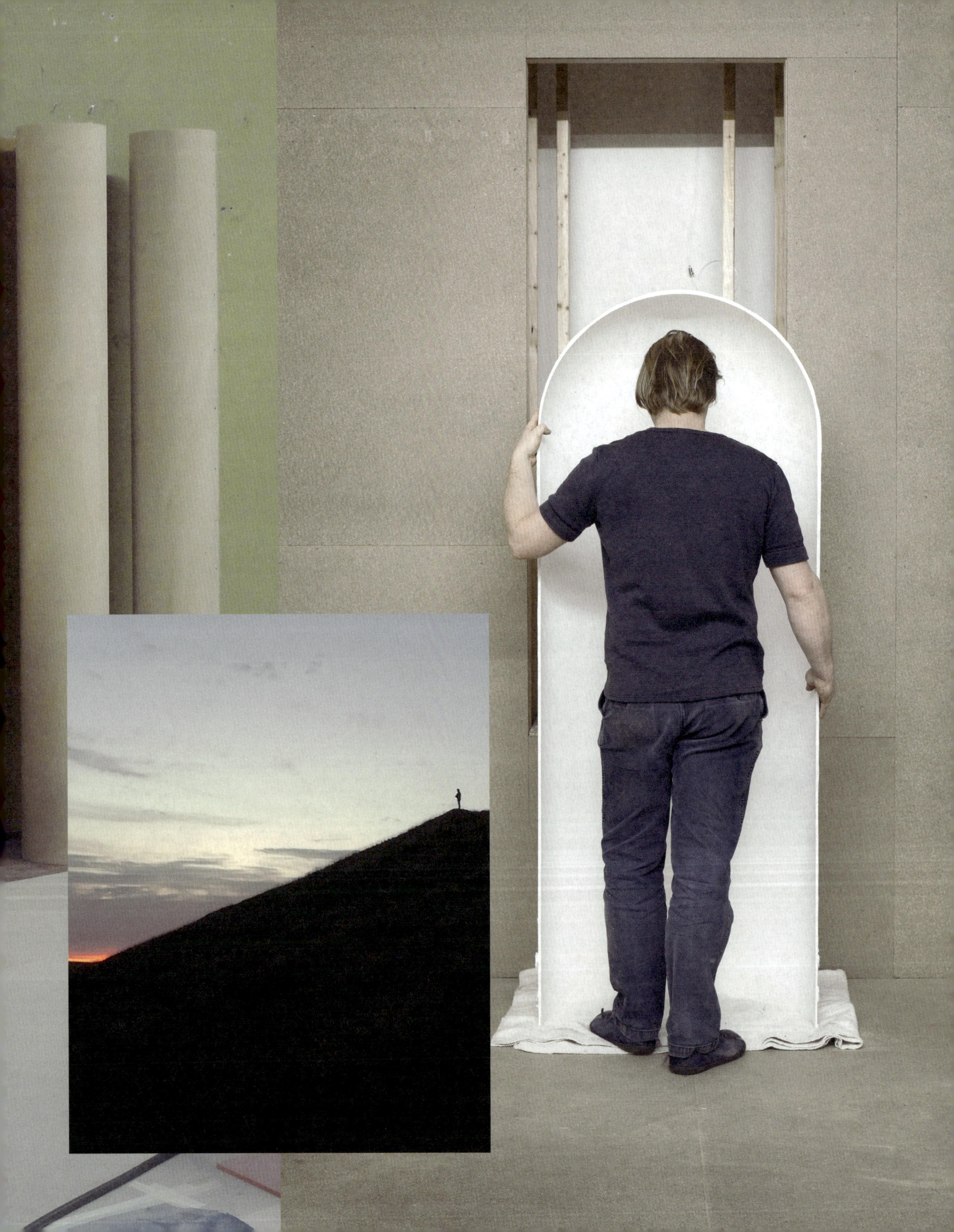

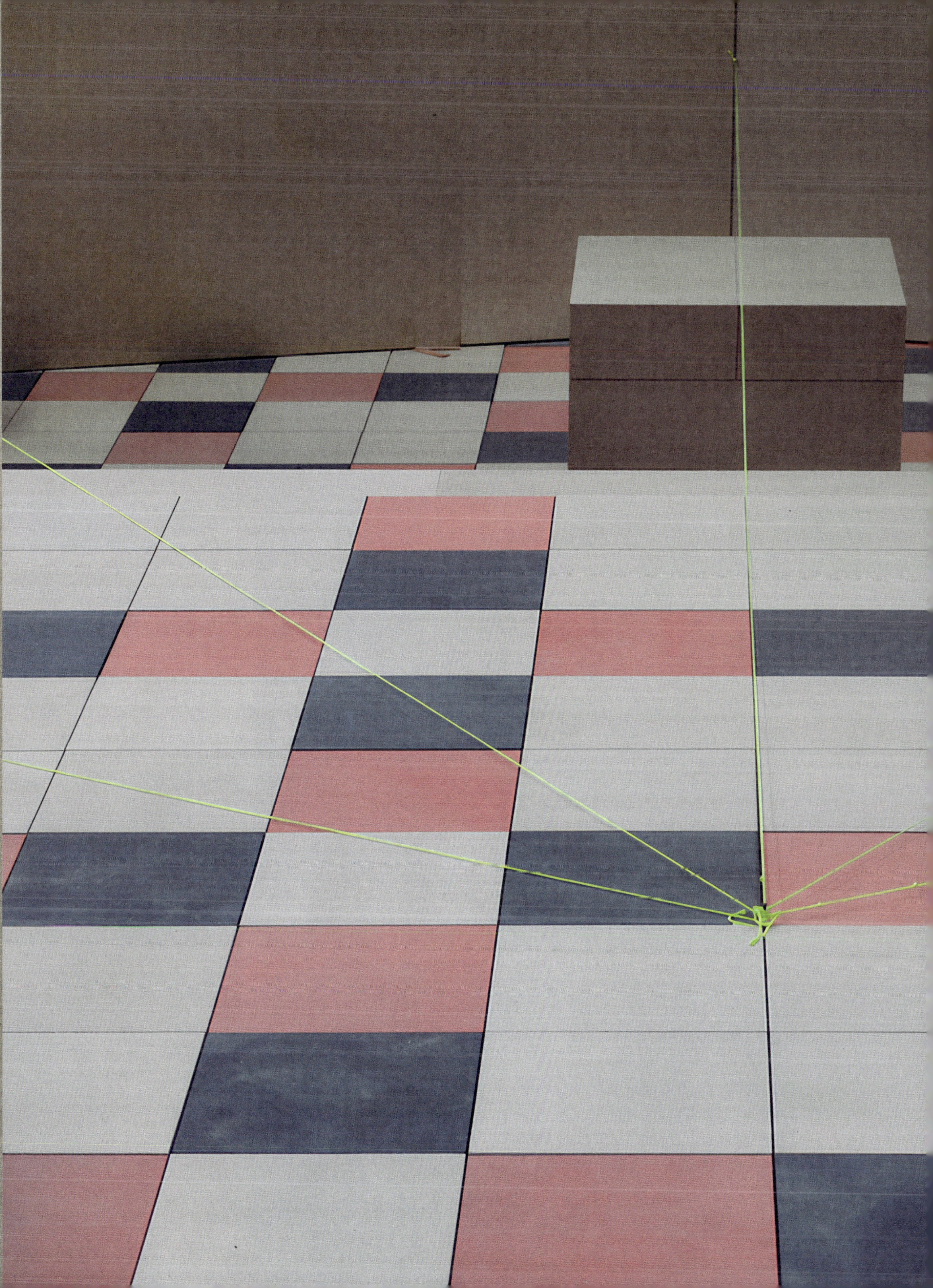

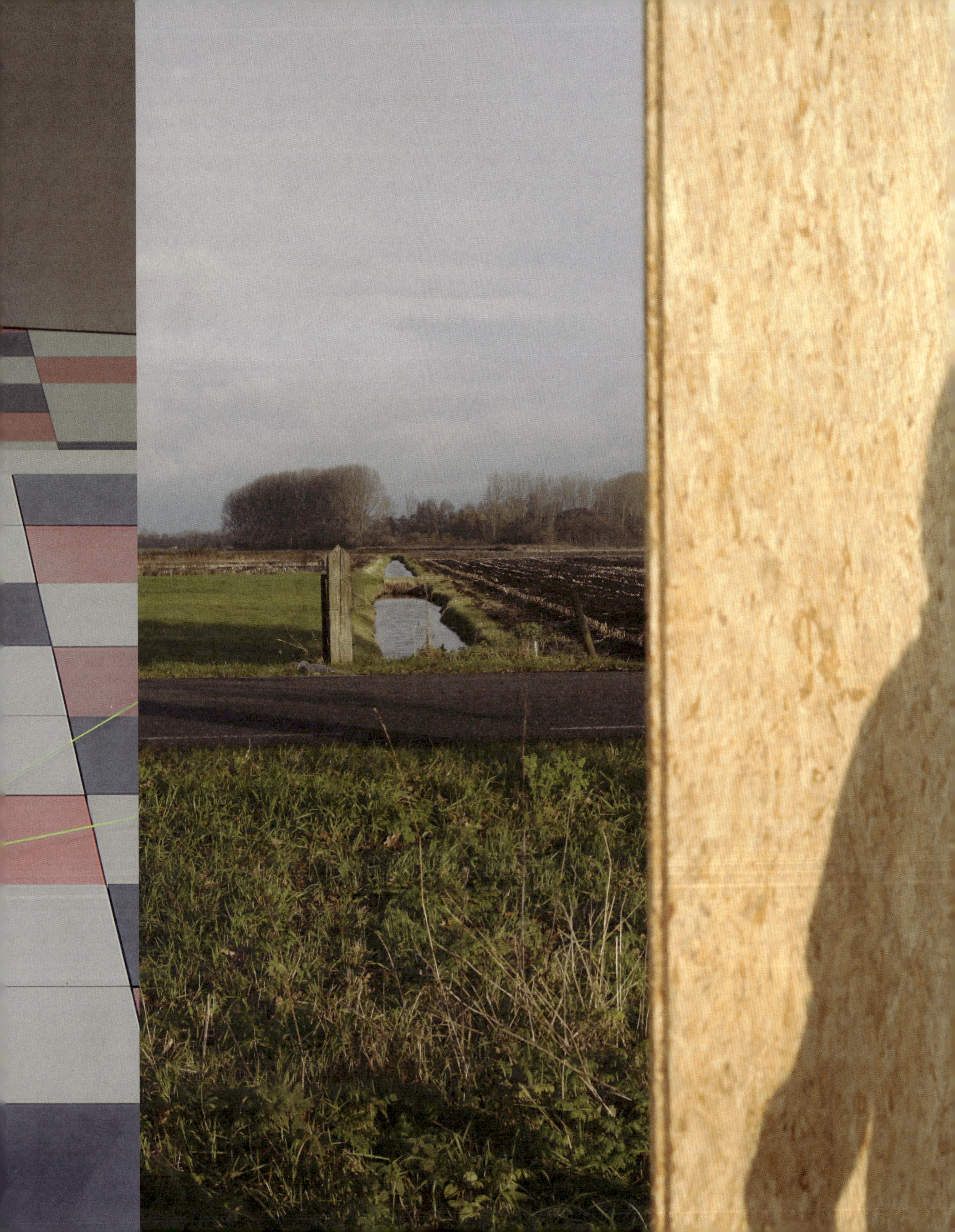

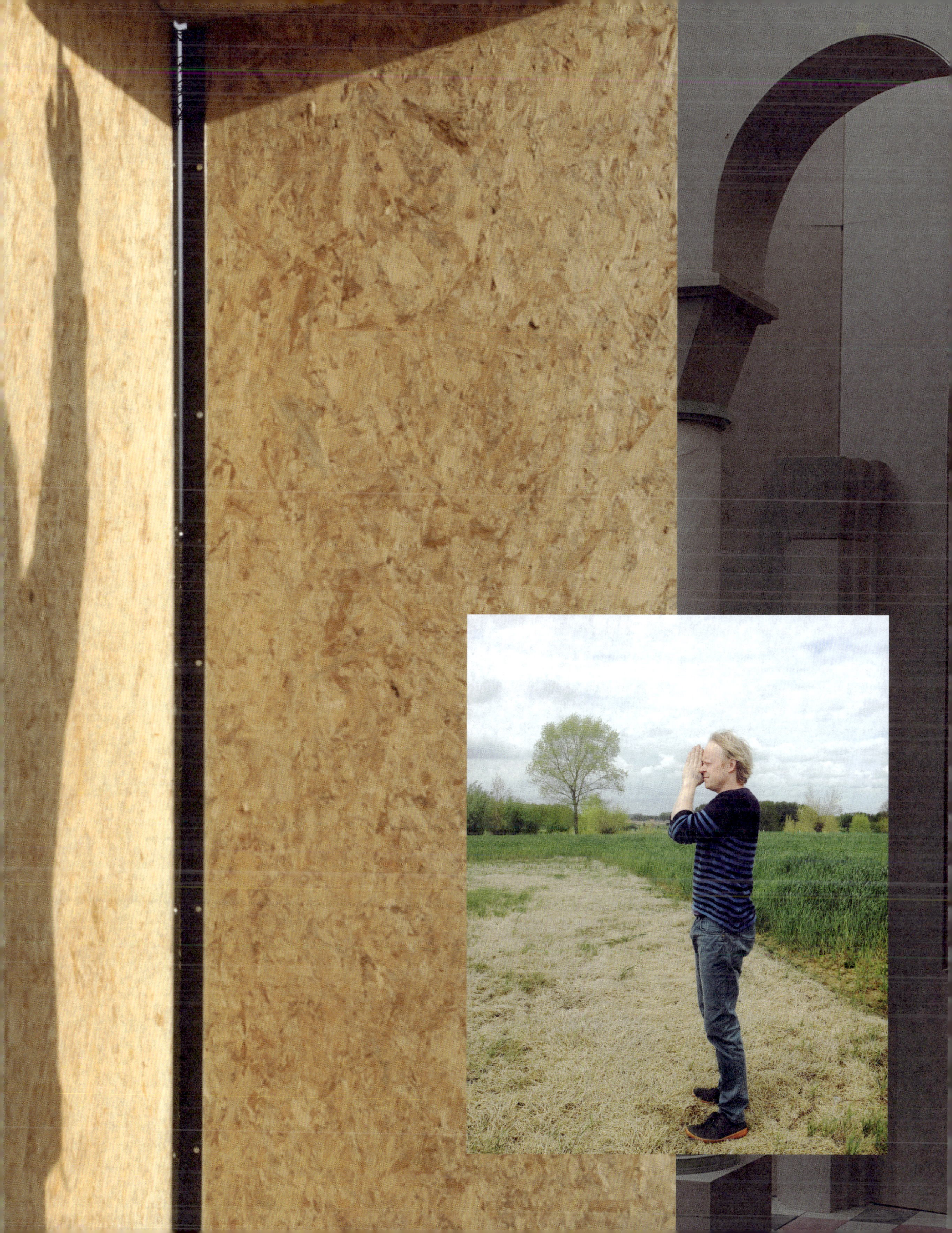

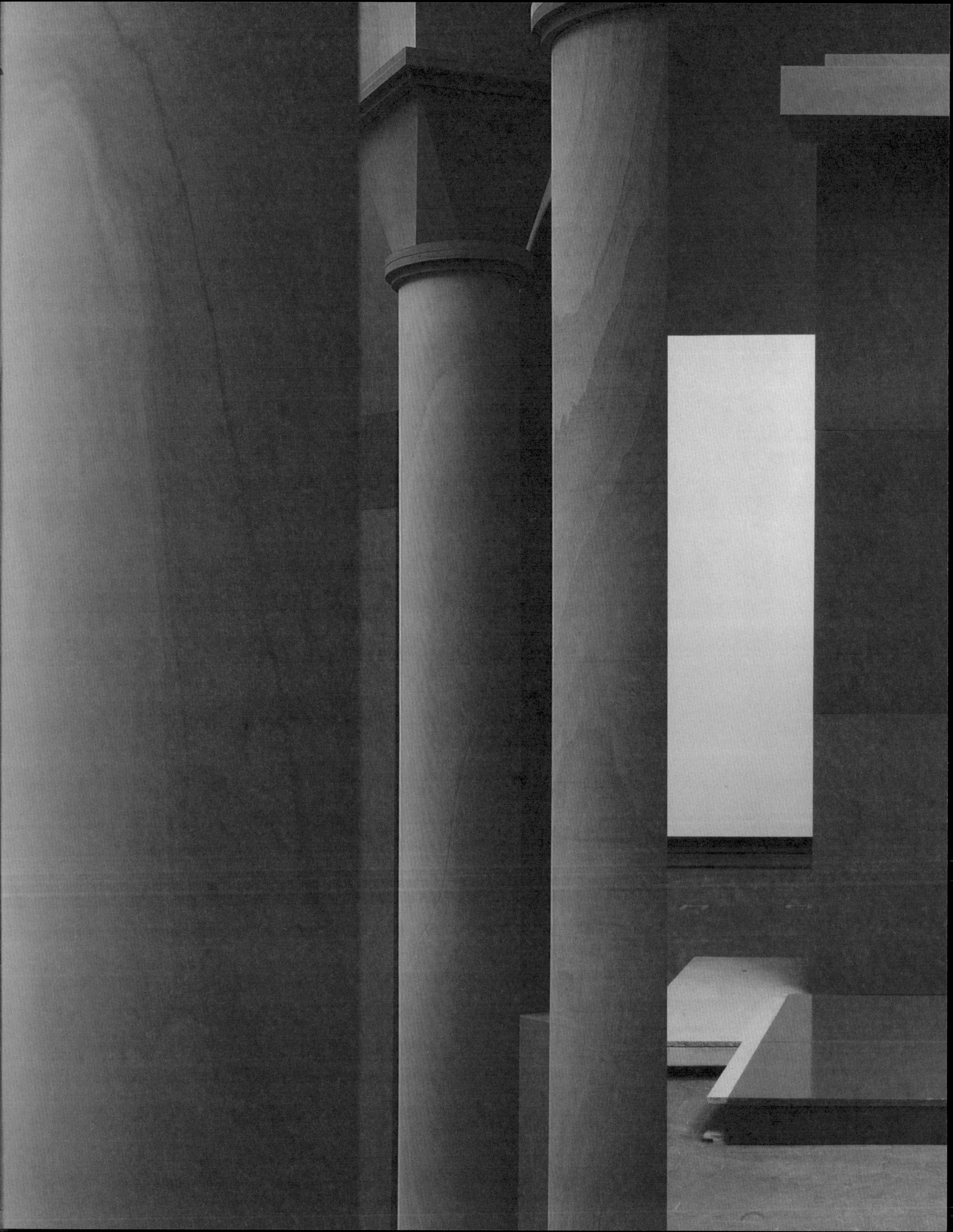

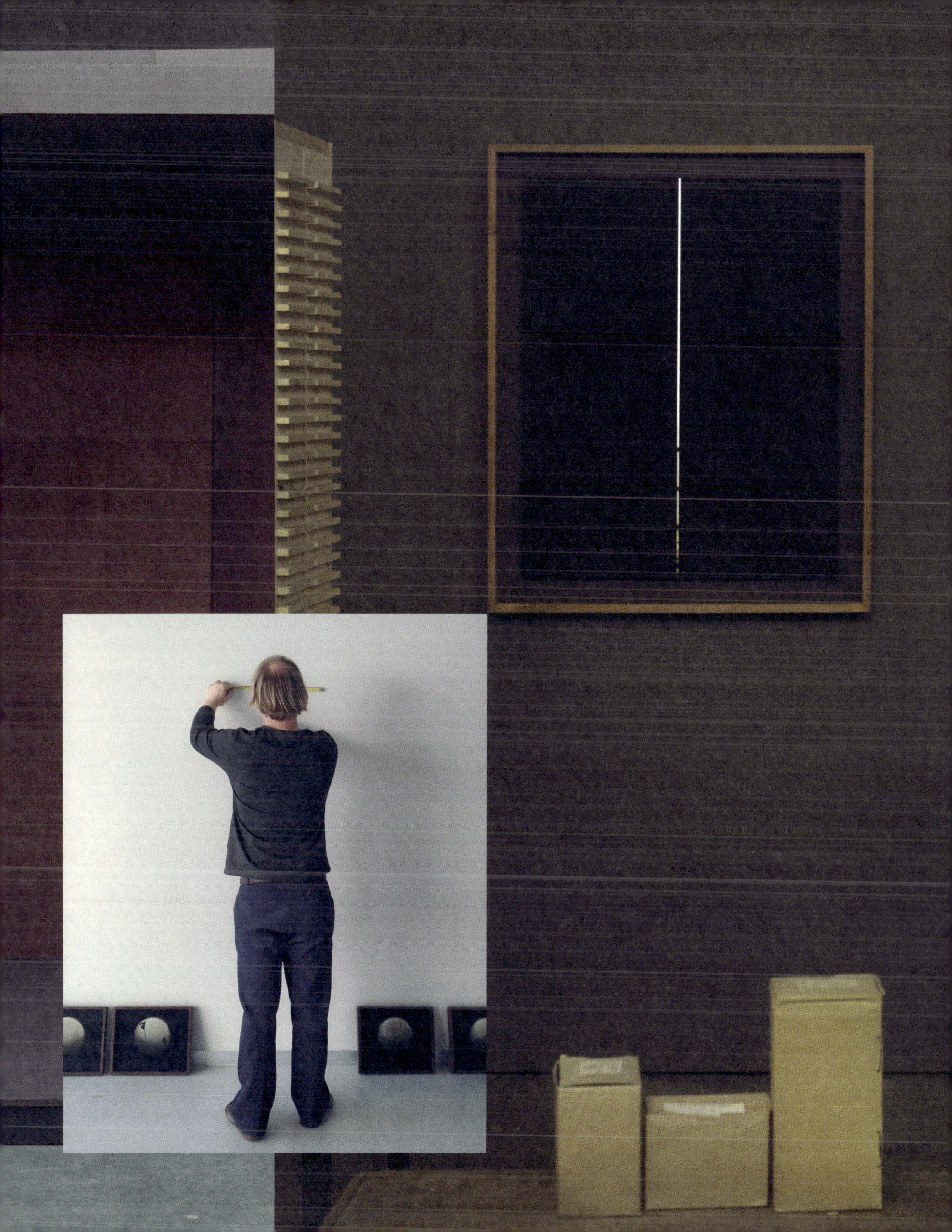

VERTICAL HORIZON

RECONSTRUCTIONS

FORENSIC SERIES

EXPO

To reveal the image, Lefere makes interventions in reality. He often uses shadow, inspired by the French philosopher Gilles Deleuze, who calls that which is hidden 'the fold of the visible'. The disappearance of the light renders the image visible. Lefere's point of departure for the series 'I never promised you a horizon' is the extremely narrow framing of a depiction of the horizon. With its promise of infinity, the horizon is hemmed in by a vertical slit. Furthermore, Lefere chooses not to set his focus on the horizon, but on the boundary between image and non-image. In this way, he keeps the viewer in suspense. The horizon beyond can only be seen in the mind's eye, and it is therefore excluded from the image – a strategy often applied by Lefere. The vertical horizon thus becomes a symbol of unattainable desire.

VERTICAL HORIZON

THE PROMISE OF WORLDS YET UNKNOWN

by Frederik Le Roy

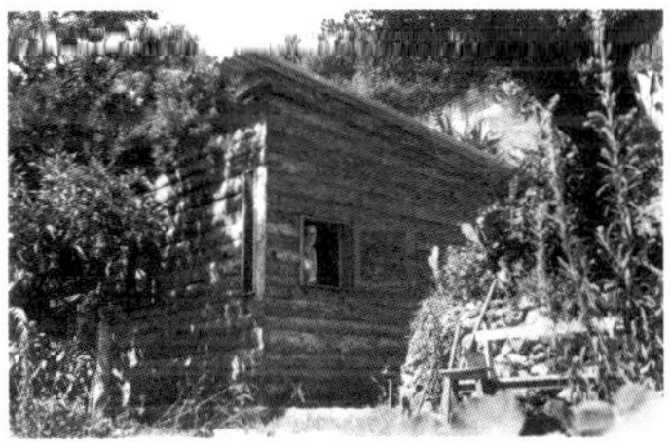

I

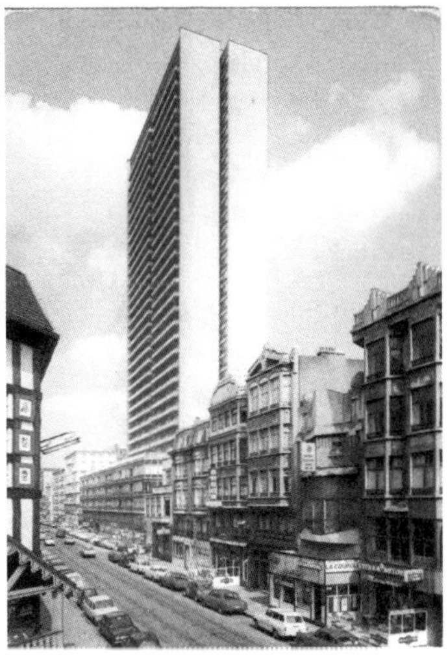

II

Suddenly I stopped. Between my eyes and the horizon a sensational event has occurred; a vertical rock, in granite, is there, upright, like a menhir: its vertical makes a right angle with the horizon. Crystallisation fixation of the site. This is a place to stop, because here is a complete symphony, magnificent relationships, nobility. The vertical gives the meaning of the horizontal. One is alive because of the other. Such are the powers of synthesis.

Le Corbusier[1]

The installation *'I never promised you a horizon'* (2014), which resulted from an artist's residency in Drente, the Netherlands, is an idiosyncratic commentary on the Romantic yearning for the landscape at the turn of the nineteenth century. The Romantics sought out sweeping, breathtaking natural views. They looked for vantage points from which the landscape unfolded before them at its most picturesque or sublime and attempted to capture their experiences in paintings or poetry. Here the photographer opts for a radically different perspective, recalling Le Corbusier's statement that 'the vertical dimension endows the horizon with significance'[(I)]. Lefere built a 'viewing device' that makes it possible to view the horizon in a novel way. In contrast with the horizontality and openness of Romantic landscape art, he invokes a vertical line, such that it is not the image but the frame that dominates. Further, Lefere always sets the focus on the middle plane of the image and not on the landscape behind it. In this way, he emphasises not the object of the looking but the frame that always and unavoidably frames that looking. In addition to the photographs taken through the viewing device, Lefere also presents an idealised wooden maquette of the viewing device, a prototype that invites the viewer to imagine other experiences of the horizon. As a posthumous homage to Le Corbusier and his insight, Lefere seeks to underscore the fact that the landscape – and by extension the horizon – is a product of the interplay between the constructed and the non-constructed. Similarly, the photographic image is always the result of the interplay between frame and object or between device and reality.

The series 'A more elevated scene (Looking West)' (2014), made for a location-specific project in Ostend, is based on a dialogue with the residential tower Residentie Europacentrum[(II)], which was built in the centre of Ostend in the latter half of the 1960s. While for many the building is a prime example of how high-rise buildings have marred Belgium's coastal landscape, for residents of the building it offers a marvellous point from which to view the sea and hinterland. The design and height of the Europacentrum call to mind the motto 'everyone has the right to a horizon' (attributed to architect Renaat Braem).

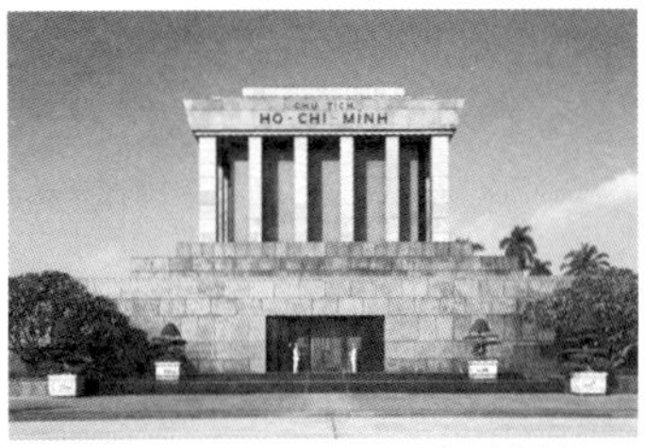

© quintinlake.com

III

However, the horizon that these residents get to enjoy is the one taken away from those living in the shadow of the tower. The panoramic restaurant on the top floor of the building was intended to partially compensate for this, but when it was forced to close in the mid-1990s due to safety concerns, this view of the horizon was once again denied.

The democratisation and/or privatisation of the horizon is a crucial theme in 'A more elevated scene (Looking West)'. At its centre is an architectural scale model that depicts the tower in its entirety as a viewing device for looking at the horizon. This intervention is intended to once again give the tower a public function as a meeting place and viewing point. With this, the artist alludes not only to the closed panoramic restaurant but also the plan – never realised – to build a theatre at the base of the tower to replace the city theatre that was demolished to make way for the tower. In this case the tower itself becomes the theatre: a black box with the purpose of visualising the boundary between sea and sky in a new way. The images that flank the maquette follow through on this idea. They suggest the tower as a viewing device that creates a specific frame for undermining archetypal landscape images, such as that of the sunset. In a number of images, there is an inversion of the vertical 'zip' (a term used by Barnett Newman to refer to the bold lines that divided the planes of colour in his paintings): for example, in a close-up of the lift that once led to the panoramic restaurant, the black frame takes the place of the visible zip and vice versa.

The basis for '*La raison des ombres*' (2015) is Ho Chi Minh's mausoleum in Hanoi, Vietnam[III]. In 1975, the body of the former communist leader and president of Vietnam was not cremated (as per his will), but rather embalmed and laid out in a publicly accessible mausoleum. The exhibited remains became the centrepiece of a posthumous cult of personality intended to bolster the newly reunited north and south. As a symbol of national unity and the eternal power of the communist state system, the mausoleum is an extremely politicised space. However, this concrete political context is not the reason why Lefere made this place the focus of a long-term project. Stripped of its historical context, Ho Chi Minh's mausoleum is a means of reflection on the status of the (photographic) image and how photography, memory and history are intertwined.

No images are available of the inside of the mausoleum, the sanctum sanctorum where the embalmed corpse of the political leader is laid out. Photography is strictly forbidden there. The ban on image-making makes this space an anomaly: a non-photographed sanctuary in an over-mediatised world. The interior space's only traces on the outside are the memories of the thousands of visitors that are guided through it daily in one fluid motion (stopping is also forbidden). Based on his own memories and scant footage from a documentary about the construction of the mausoleum, Lefere built a 1:3 scale wooden reconstruction in his studio. This abstracted reconstruction was subsequently photographed – a process he also employed in previous work to depict places where photography was prohibited.

Like a number of the images from 'A more elevated scene' and 'I never promised you a horizon', La raison des ombres is what W.J.T. Mitchell called a meta-image – an image that reflects on the image. While in the two prior image series the zip or

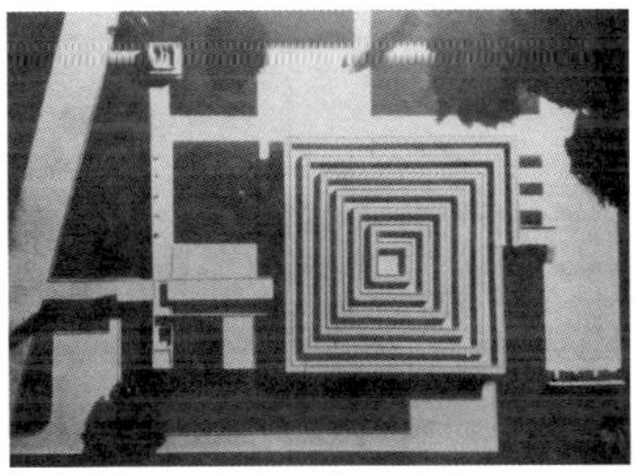

IV

vertical horizon makes a theme of the boundary between frame and image, La raison des ombres facilitates a meditation on the photographic image and on temporality. In 1924 Stalin is alleged to have claimed, in a speech following the death of his predecessor, that the communist body does not decompose. This before ordering that Lenin's corpse be forever preserved in the manner of the Egyptian pharaohs. Herein lies the link with photography. The photographic image freezes time. Just as mummification denies the transience of the body and thus the progress of time, the image embalms reality. The mausoleum is transformed into a camera obscura. At the same time, the Ho Chin Minh Mausoleum, where no photographic souvenir may be created, is a place where the image both appears and disappears.

Although the space may appear dark and dismal – it is, after all, a place where life is fixed – it does at least incorporate a possible point of escape. The wall of the mausoleum has a vertical slice cut out of it, offering a liberating view of the outside. Here Lefere once again takes inspiration from Le Corbusier, who in the late 1930s drew up a (never realised) plan for the Museum of Unlimited Extension[(IV)], in which the viewer is led along a labyrinthine trail with the occasional section cut out of the wall, offering a view out to the surrounding landscape.

This brings us to an aspect of the horizon that plays a role in each of the works in this exhibition. French philosopher Louis Marin noted in 1973 that the horizon has become an ambiguous concept in modernity. 'Oddly enough', he writes in Utopics: Spatial Play, 'horizon, which originally meant a limit, the power of circumscribing a place, connotes at the end, immensity, infinity.' In addition to being a limit, the horizon holds the promise of worlds yet unknown. This is how Marin associates the horizon with the workings of a utopia. And it is precisely this ambiguity that frequently appears in these photos and that connects the geometry of the horizon as a play of lines and perspectives with the horizon as the promise of, and the desire for, that which lies elusively beyond our perception.

This text was previously published as an accompaniment to the solo exhibition '*I never promised you a horizon*' at Casa Argentaurum in Ghent in 2015.

1. from a 1929 lecture about a hike along the coast of Britain

I https://capmoderne.com/media/uploads/2015/06/20/cabanon-archi-02.jpg
II https://www.deplate.be/nl/postkaart-europacentrum-van-iseghemlaan-0
III https://www.quintinlake.com/image/I0000UbvWB1VJasA
IV https://evolutionaryurbanism.com/wp-content/uploads/2017/02/20170220_182031.jpg

I NEVER PROMISED YOU A HORIZON

2014-2015

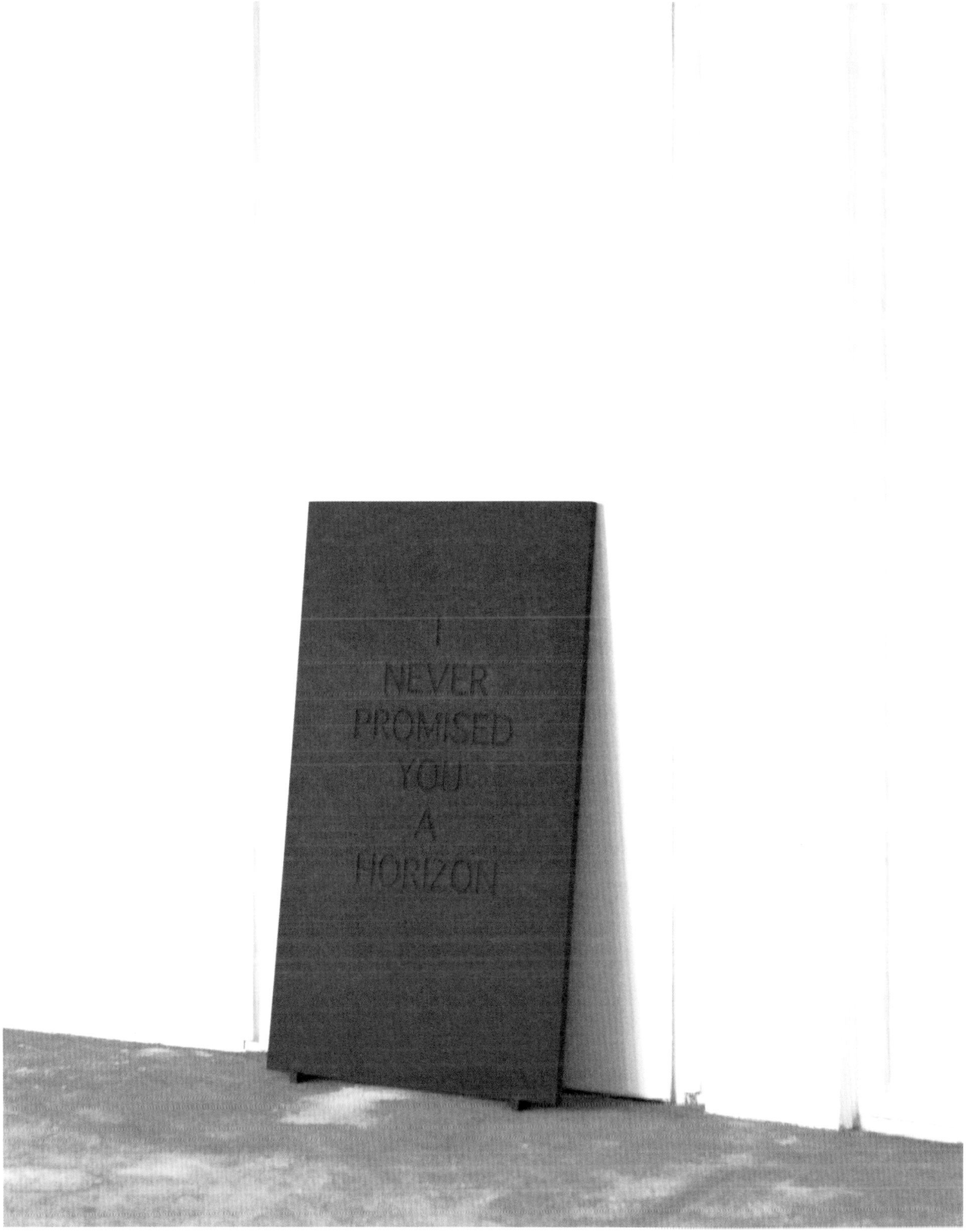

Inscription

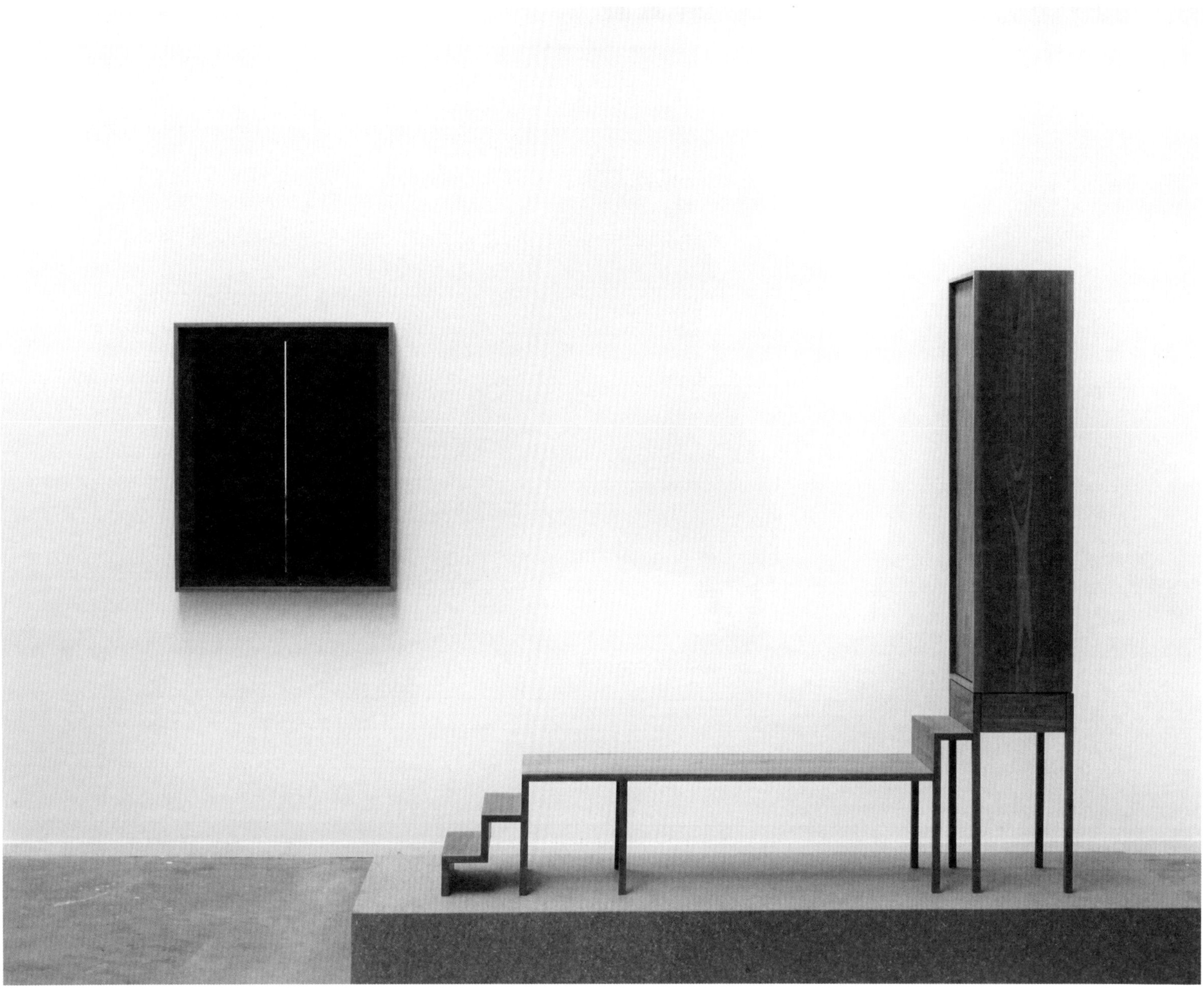

Model

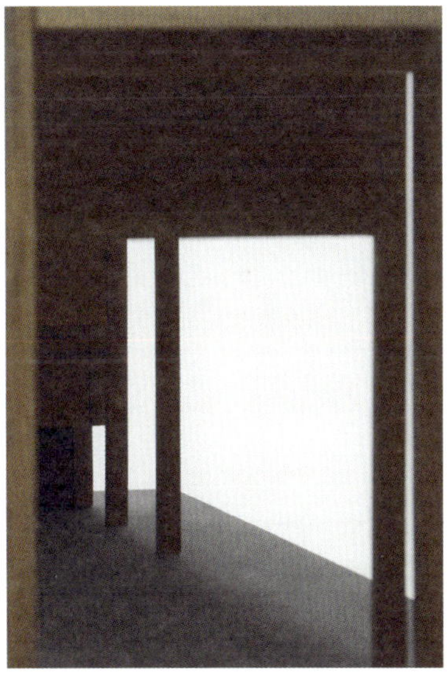

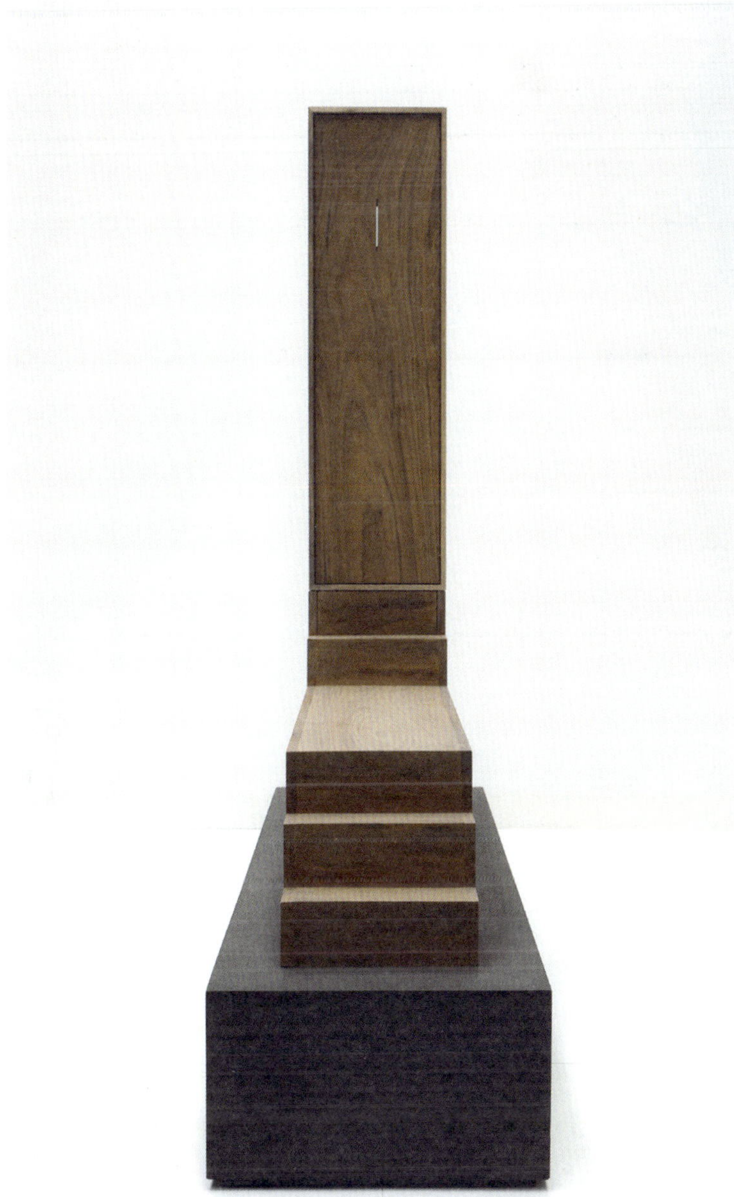

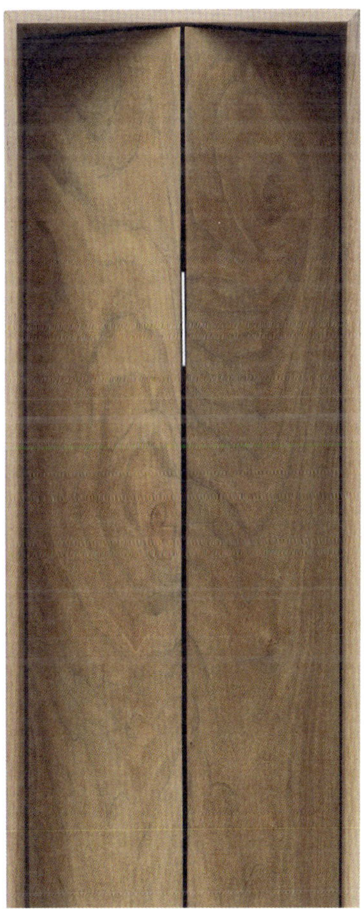

Horizon I

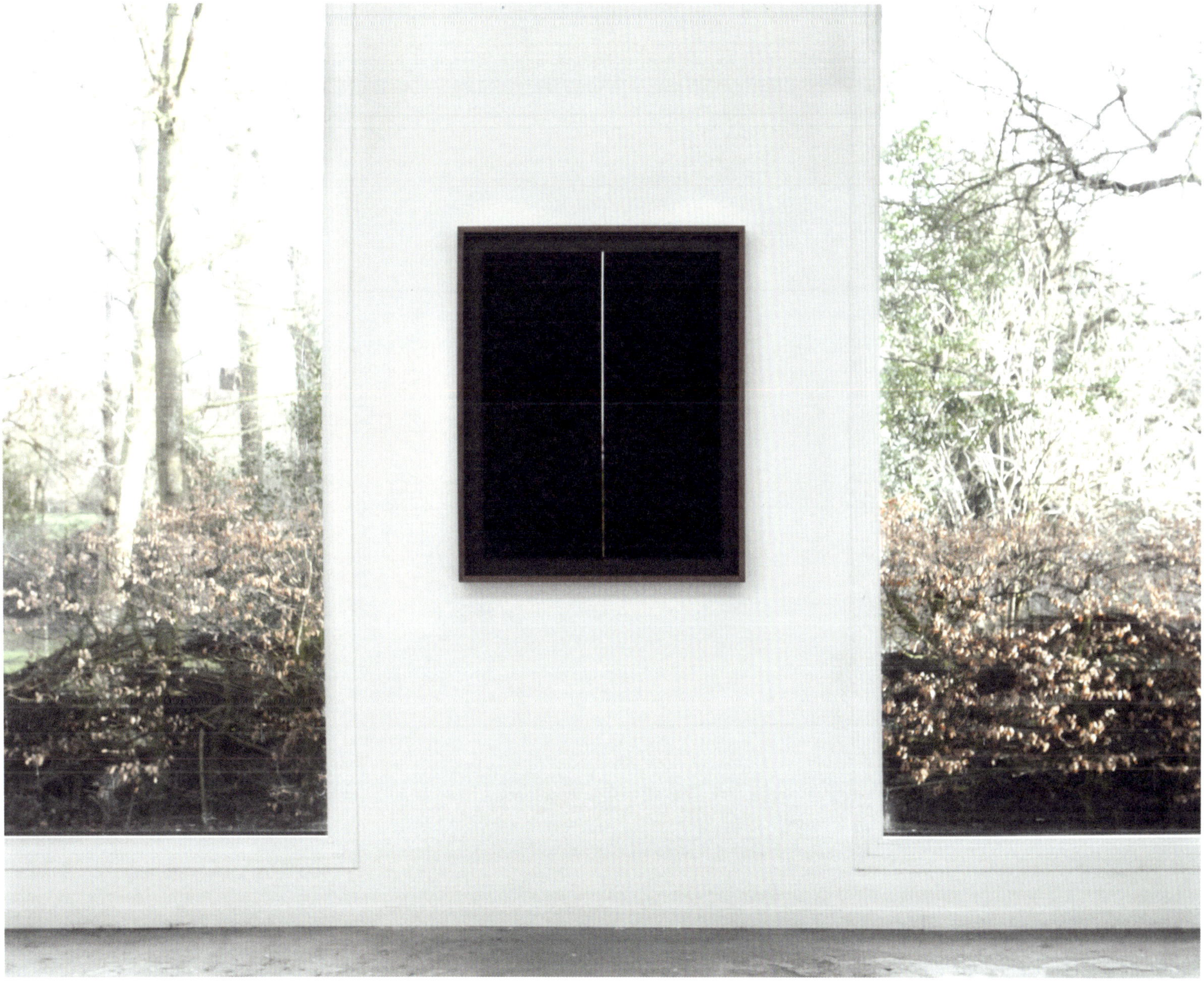

Horizon IV   Horizon V

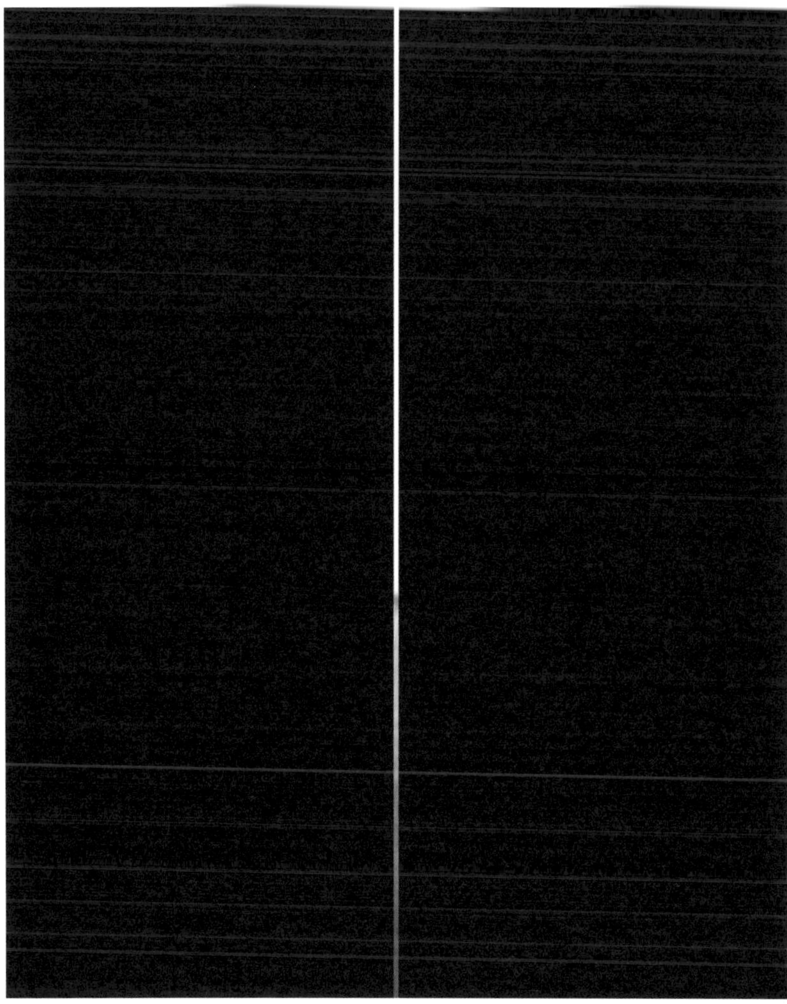

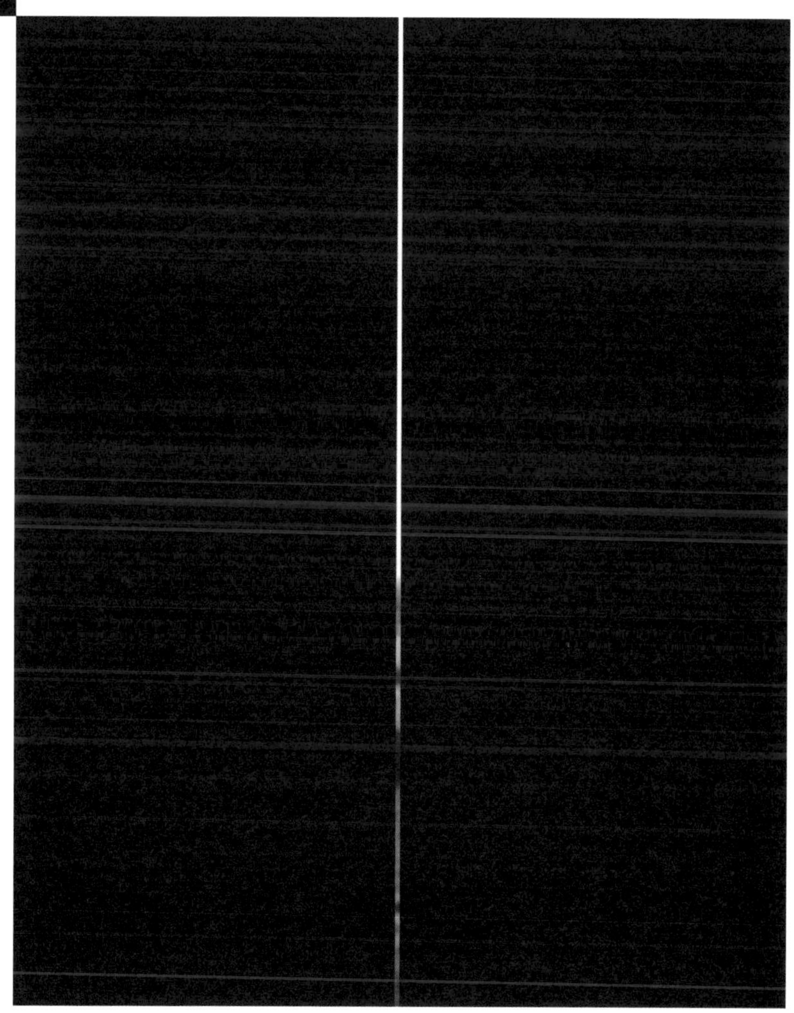

Horizon VI Horizon VII

A MORE ELEVATED SCENE (LOOKING WEST)

2014

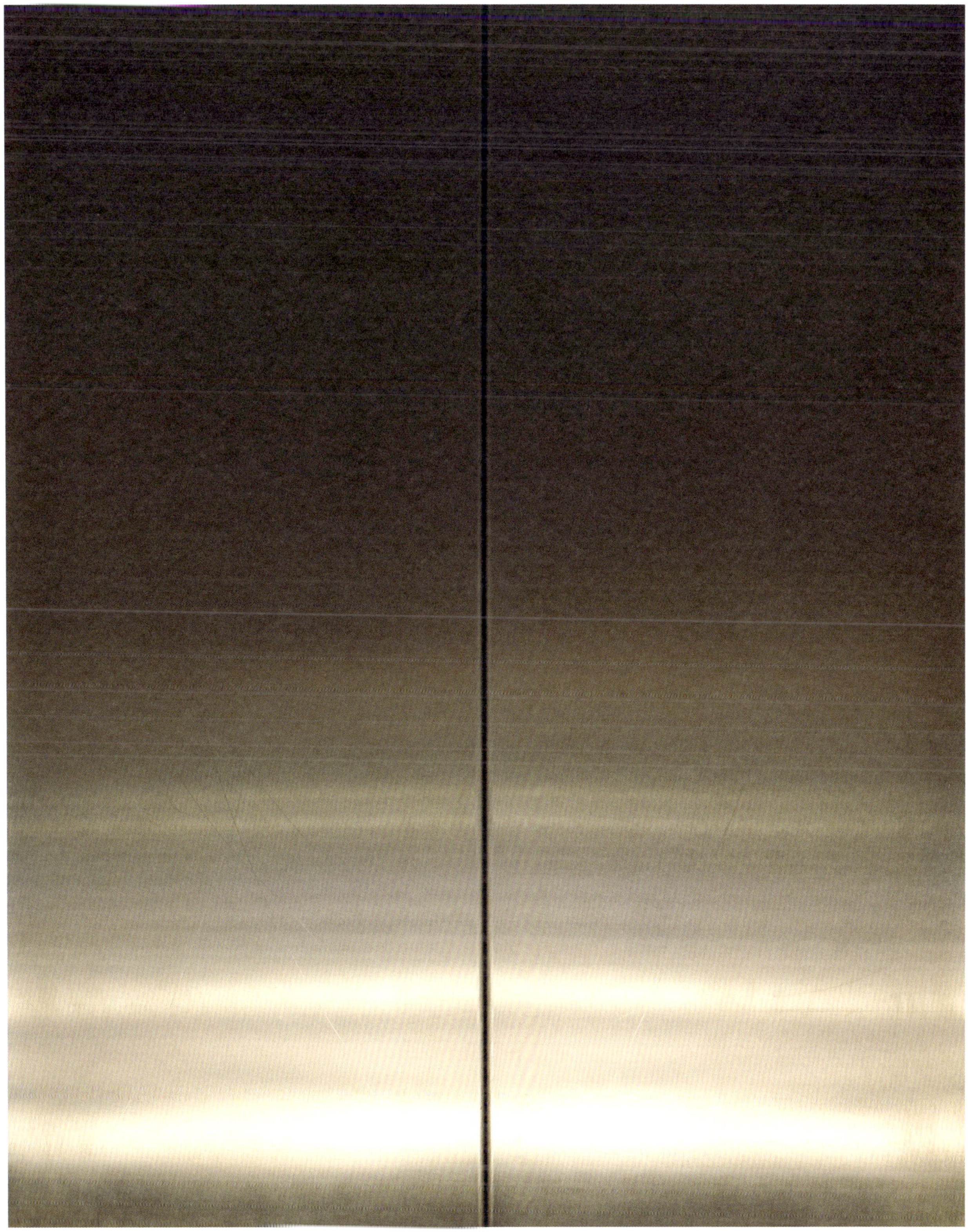

Golden dawn (reversed)

Horizon

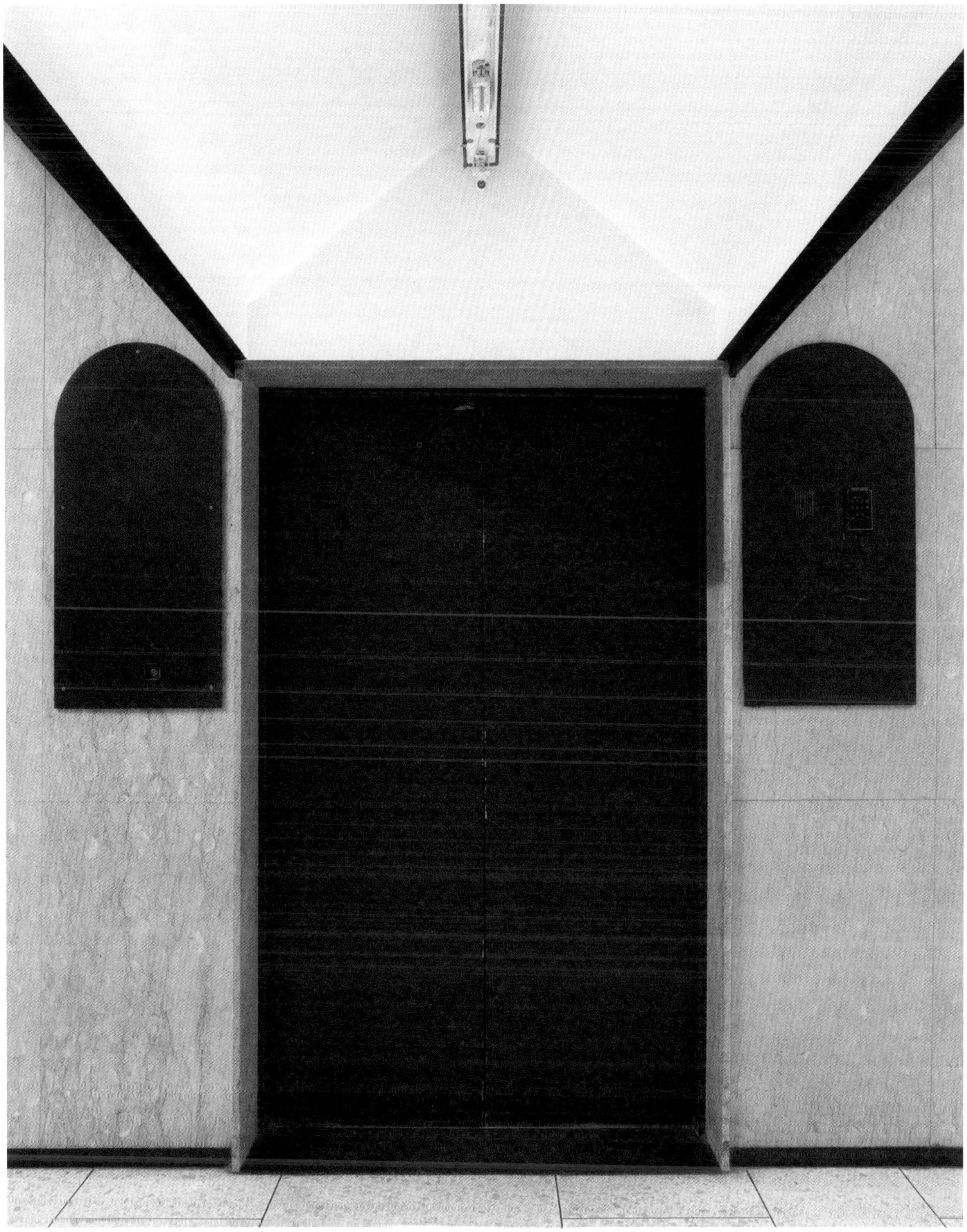

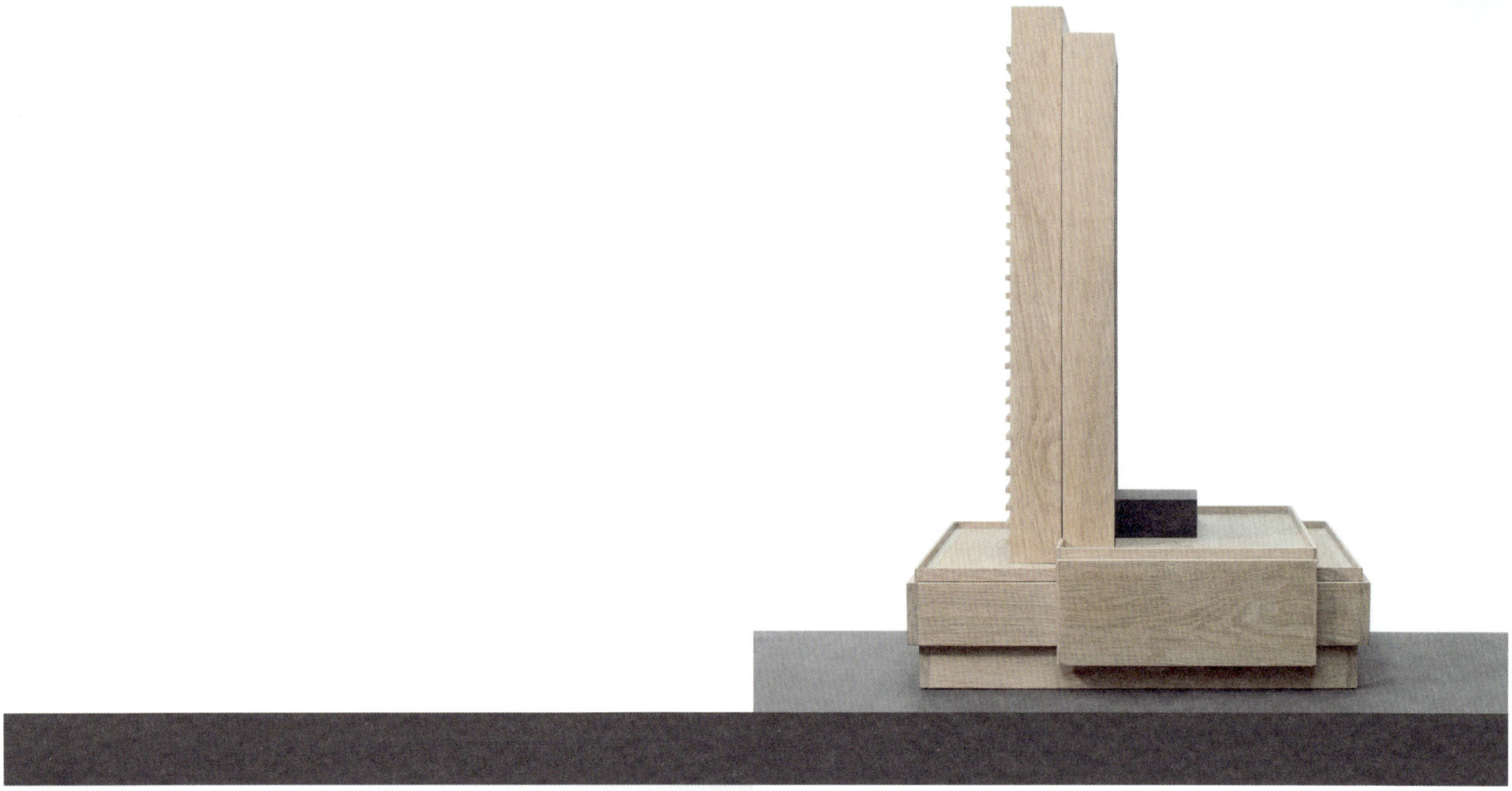

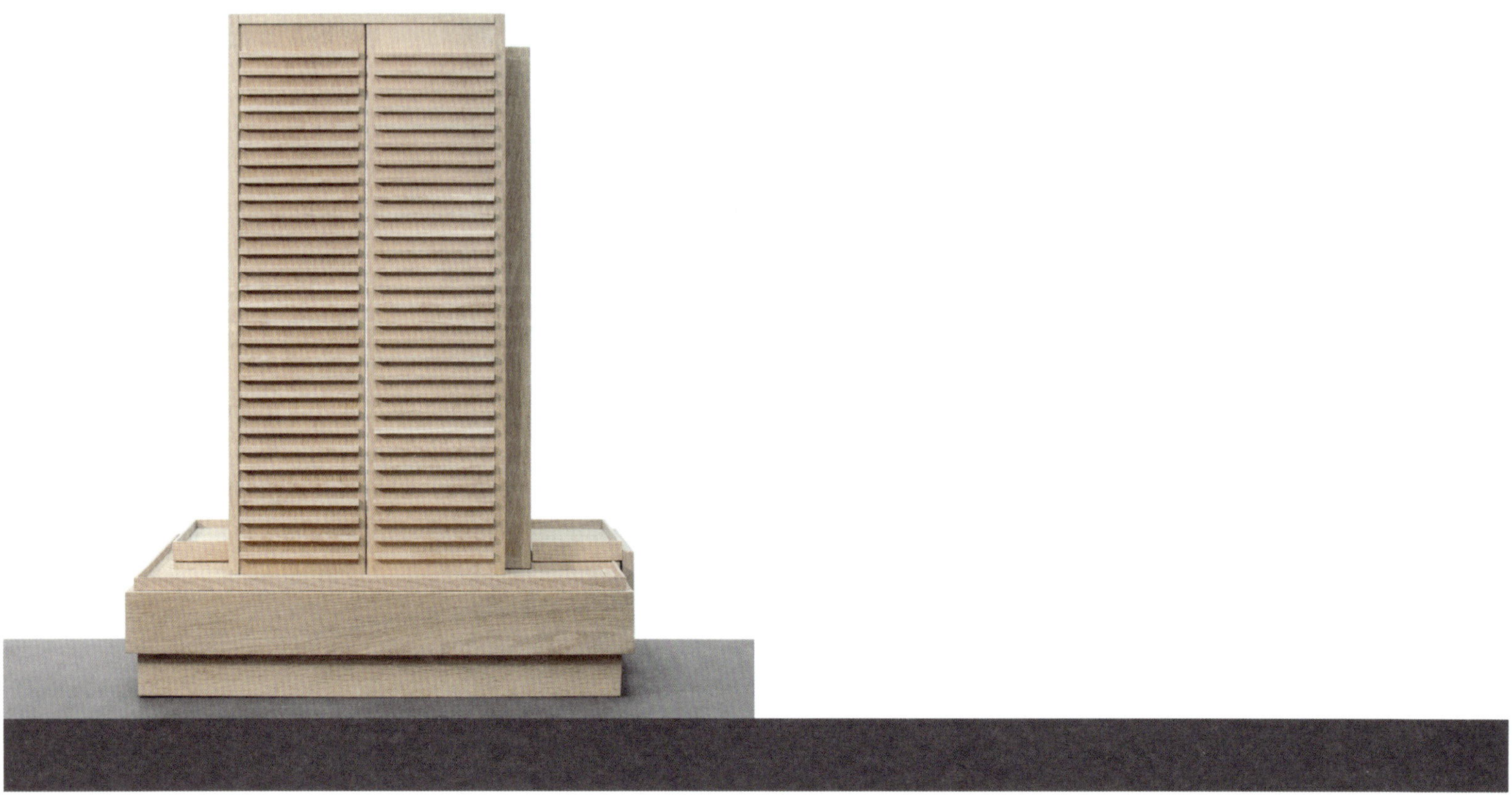

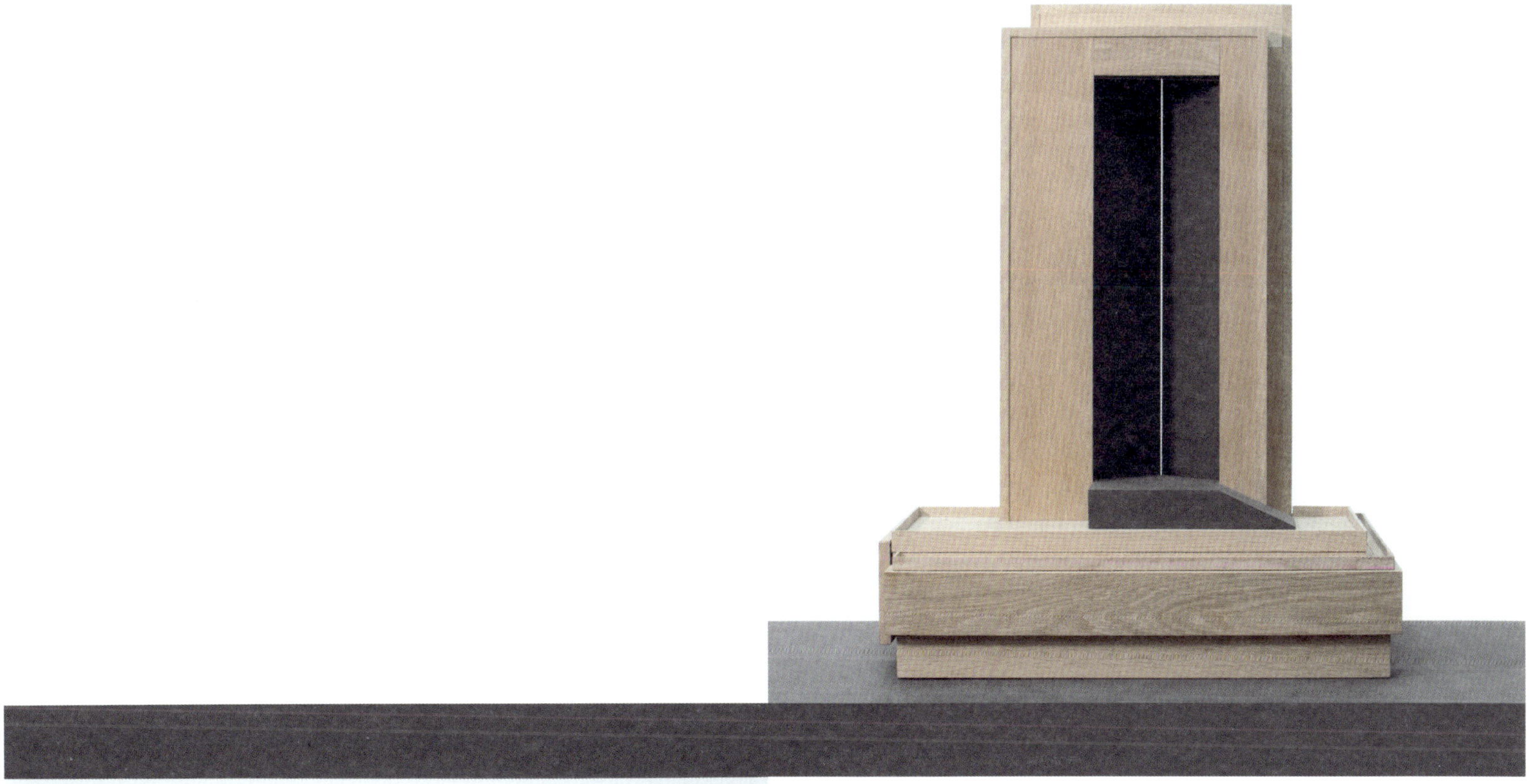

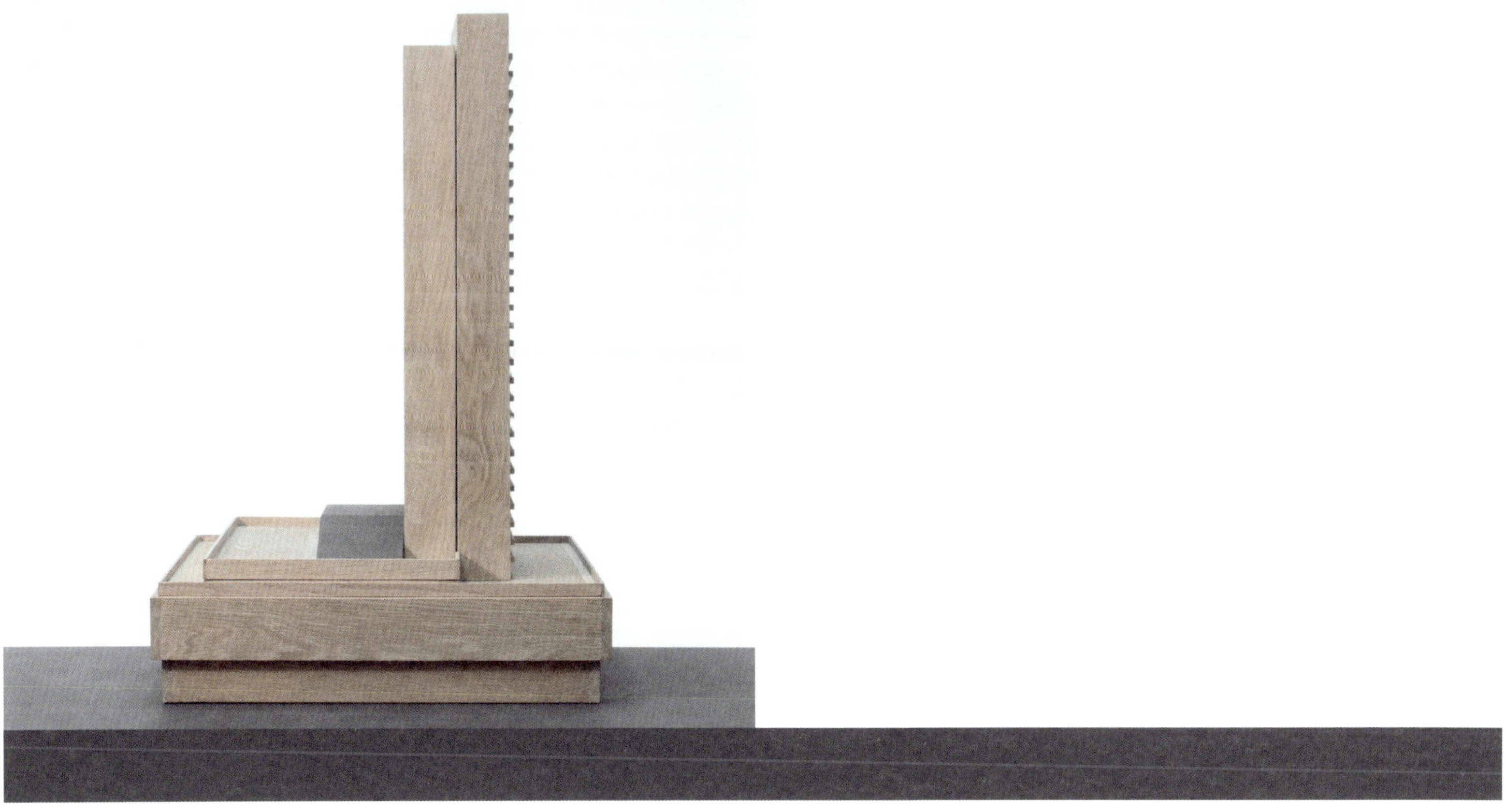

Reconstructions are a common thread in Lefere's work. He builds sets and scenes based on existing rooms, spaces or architectural elements – often from memory. These reconstructions usually serve as the basis for photographs. They are an essential part of his artistic process. Similarly to how a scientist utilises reference models, Lefere uses his reconstructions in the consideration of scale, framing and lighting – the elements he uses to carefully construct his images. Sometimes the reconstructions disappear and only the image remains. In other cases, they continue to evolve and become autonomous works. The planning and construction of these reconstructions often takes several months. This protracted process results in extremely layered images that are charged with significance and require patience to decipher. They are the antithesis of what we usually associate with photography: more monument than moment, more a constructed intention than a slice of life. Simultaneously cryptic, evocative and alienating.

RECONSTRUCTIONS

AVEC LA RAISON DES OMBRES ET MIROIRS

by Tim Vanheers

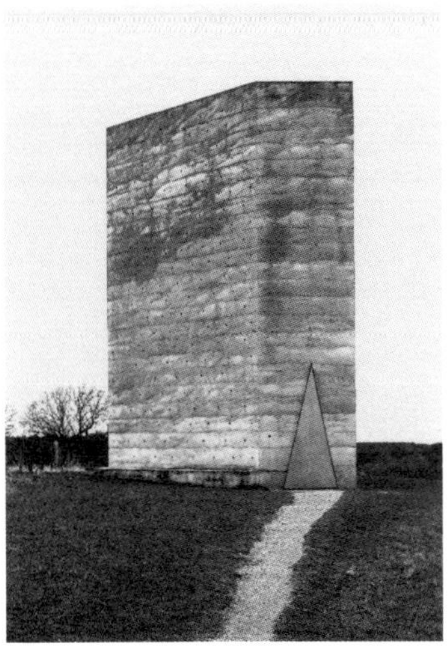

I

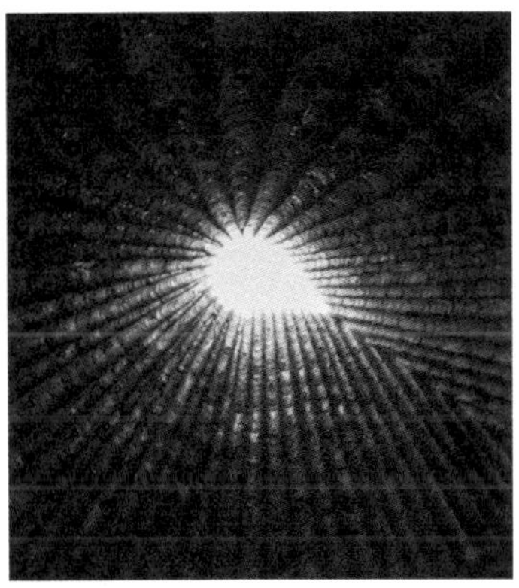

II

On my journey through the Eifel, I made a stop in the small village of Wachendorf. There in its fields lies the Bruder Klaus Chapel[I-II], a famous work by the architect Peter Zumthor. A great many pilgrims of architecture wend their way to this chapel every year. I have booked accommodation nearby so as to avoid the masses. At the crack of dawn, I make my way through the fields. In the distance I spot a boxy form that I recognise from the photos. I imagine how the interior of this remarkable place will look. Having arrived, I open the unique triangular door and enter. What follows is a remarkable experience. What I had imagined does not correspond with the reality. The inside of the chapel looks completely different than I had expected: narrower, taller, more organic and more intimate. Light filters in sparsely through the oculus, while a number of candles provide a warm glow. I allow my eyes to feast, my thoughts to roam. Time glides by. Then the door suddenly opens and I hear the voices of other visitors. Daylight floods in abruptly, interrupting my reverie. After what seems like an eternity, I return to the outdoors. I look at my watch. Barely ten minutes have passed since I entered.

In his book Atmospheres, Zumthor writes about architectonic quality. Over the course of his career, he has attempted to 'design' experiences such as the one I had in the Bruder Klaus Chapel. He reconstructs an 'atmosphere' from his memories, which he attempts to impart on the building through the decisions he makes in the architectural design process. It is this 'atmosphere', something fairly elusive and subjective, that touches people when they experience a building by Zumthor.

In his photography, Lieven Lefere is like an architect. He constructs his images from elements such as scale and framing, sculpting with light and shadow. Sometimes his process prompts him to literally start building, reconstructing places as he remembers them. These intermediary constructions rarely remain standing, however. What counts for him is the image, the photo. That is all that remains.

Just like the buildings of Peter Zumthor, Lefere's photos have an elusive quality to them. And just as Zumthor attempts to (re)construct a certain atmosphere, Lefere (re)constructs situations and places from a memory, idea or mental image. The memory of an objective reality is carefully built up from scratch, acquiring a new layeredness in the process. Lefere is meticulous in this, taking a great, long run-up to the final photo (just as the Swiss architect, who is said to have devoted nine years to his chapel project). Lefere is not so much interested in representing objective reality. His interest lies more in conveying the subjective, which he does by carefully manipulating all the parameters that make the photo what it is.

Take light and shadow, for example. In Lefere's photographs, light is practically a character in itself. It even seems charged with significance, like the air in a cathedral. And shadow is at least as prominent. Lefere is a master obscurer. He is aware that shadow evokes certain interpretations. As Jun'ichirō Tanizaki describes in his essay In Praise of Shadows, we in the West are obsessed with our quest for ever more light. To us, shadow is somehow suspect. We perceive that which unfolds in the shadows as ambiguous. It is this ambiguity that Lefere plays upon in his work.

In Six Memos for the Next Millennium (a text that Zumthor refers to in Thinking Architecture), Italo Calvino describes the connotations of the Italian word vago. (...) Italian is, I believe, the only language in which the word for 'vague' (vago) also means charming, attractive; having originally

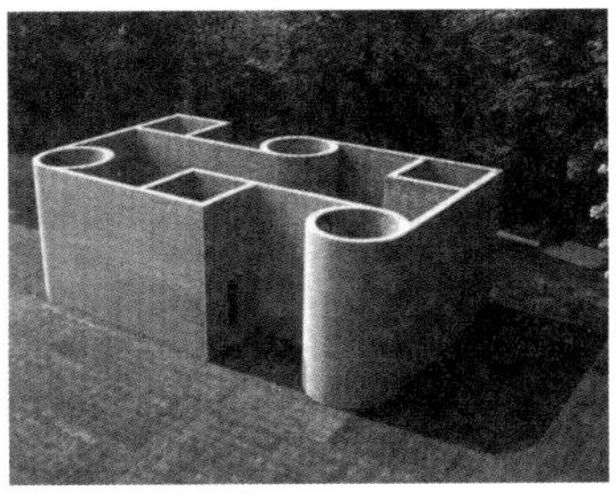

III

meant 'wandering', it still carries with it a feeling of movement and mutability, which in Italian suggests not only uncertainty and indeterminacy but also grace and pleasure.

If light captures and objectifies, then shadow brings vagueness and thus space for movement and subjective interpretation. In the work of Lieven Lefere, this vagueness seems ever present. The shadows are rich with texture, the light is never absolute. There are obscuring elements that elicit questions from the viewer. The complete overview is limited. Not everything is revealed.

Often there are even elements that the viewer cannot see at all. We don't know what hides behind the wooden doors in Nothing is more visible than Things hidden. We can only guess at the landscapes in the series I never promised you a horizon. We don't know the depth of the ditches in the Hollow series, what hides beneath the tarpaulin in Hole or what the objects in the Skulls series contain. And it is precisely this same technique that Zumthor uses in his buildings. In Thinking Architecture he refers to a sculpture in the shape of a house by Per Kirkeby[(III)].

The house had no entrance. Its interior was inaccessible and hidden. It remained a secret, which added an aura of mystical depth to the sculpture's other qualities. I think that the hidden structures and constructions of a house should be organized in such a way that they endow the body of the building with a quality of inner tension and vibration.

Lefere plays masterfully with the tension between inside and outside. The viewer's gaze is partially locked out, such that the images take on an enormous suspense. The viewer knows that they will never fully fathom the image, but they keep looking. Sometimes this tension between letting in and locking out becomes the subject of the image, as in Nothing is more visible than Things hidden or La Raison des ombres. Both works depict the mausoleum of the communist leader Ho Chi Minh in Hanoi. Or, so it seems. What we see in the photo is actually a wooden reconstruction built by Lefere himself, based on his memories and footage from a documentary on the construction of the mausoleum. There are in fact no photos of the interior spaces. Photography is, after all, forbidden in this sanctum sanctorum, where the embalmed remains of Ho Chi Minh are kept. Although thousands of visitors visit the mausoleum each day, image-taking of any kind is forbidden. While in Nothing is more visible than Things hidden the building is shown from the outside, La Raison des ombres is photographed from the inside. In one image we stand outside but do not see what is inside, in the other we stand inside and do not see the outside environment. In both works we, as viewers, are locked out. But it is precisely what cannot be seen that gives the photos their 'inner tension and vibration', to use the words of Zumthor. In this way, the two photos touch upon the essence of the mausoleum, without showing it explicitly.

Like the buildings of Peter Zumthor, Lefere's works seem to exist outside of time. There is not a soul to be seen in them, nor are there any artefacts or symbols that would readily allow the viewer to put a date to the image. Time itself is shrouded. Lefere often captures multiple moments in one image or works with a very slow shutter speed. This serves to make the light more tangible and the resulting image more painterly, like a moment that is stretched out endlessly. Yet time is not the subject of his photos so much as it is in, for example, the work of Hiroshi Sugimoto. In Lefere's work it is more the absence of time that is felt. It is rather the ephemeral that looms from the shadows. The subjects chosen by Lefere are a mausoleum,

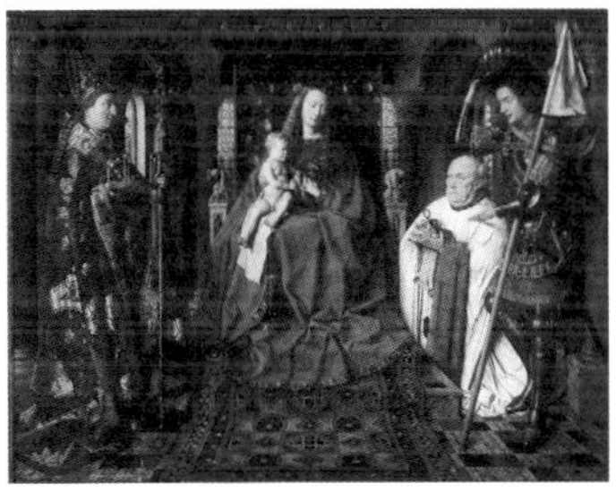

IV

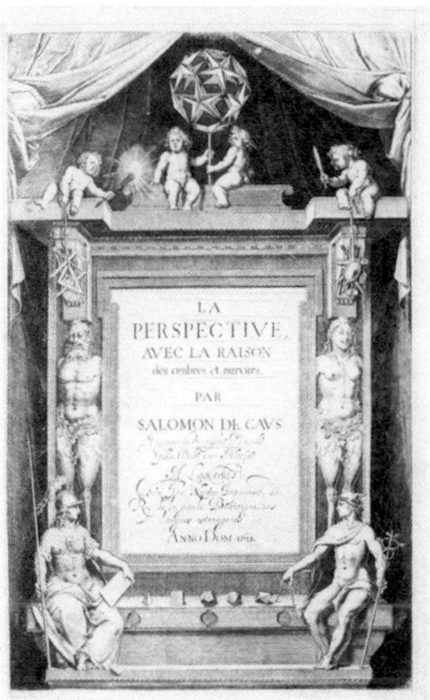

V

a mass grave, a Neolithic burial ground: places where death reigns and we are made aware of our mortality. Now consider the Skulls series, made by Lefere in collaboration with Dr. Martin Smith, professor in forensic and biological anthropology at Bournemouth University. In it we see synthetic simulations of skulls, made out of hard polyurethane to resemble bone. These objects are used in archaeology to research the violent impact of crossbows or modern bullets. They are reconstructions of brutalities, as it were: hi-tech imitations based on ancient scenarios but made in a sterile, scientific environment. Lefere photographs them as heavenly bodies set against a dark firmament, a multitude of memento mori hanging in silence, a futuristic take on 17th-century still lifes.

Scale is another of those architectural tools that Lefere uses so deftly. The monumental dimensions of some works allow one to approach them from a distance. Once in front of the photo you almost feel an urge to step into it, to enter the scene. Lefere achieves this effect by presenting his décors at a scale that is as realistic as possible and by photographing them from such a perspective that the image seems an extension of our gaze. This way the viewer can project themselves into the image. In the case of the Skulls, this can be taken quite literally: they are photographed at their true scale. And Lefere places them exactly at skull height. In La Raison des Miroirs, Lefere explores scale and perspective. Based on the doctoral research of architect Patrick Seurinck, he reconstructed the space that is depicted in Jan van Eyck's Virgin and Child with Canon van der Paele (1436)[IV]. He then took a photo of it. The result evokes a sense of both familiarity and alienation in the viewer. The omission of the characters from the famous painting leaves room for a new reading of the image, while the large scale gives the photo a certain monumentality.

In his reconstruction, Lefere was, like an archaeologist, left to interpret and fill in the gaps. The effect of the shadows and the 'infini' in the background are a direct nod to van Eyck, as is the subtle touch of glistening varnish painted on the column by Lefere to further enforce the illusion of spatiality. Then there is also his inscription on the steps: 'Avec la raison des ombres et miroirs', a reference to the book *La perspective, avec la raison des ombres et miroirs* (Perspective with the reason of shadows and mirrors, 1916) by Salomon de Caus[V]. It gives a hint of Lefere's motivations for being so obsessive in the creation of this work.

'*Avec la raison des ombres et miroirs*': it could be the title of a Lieven Lefere retrospective. For his oeuvre reconciles reason and subjectivity in an almost entirely reconstructed illusion. In frankly brilliant compositions in which nothing is what it seems. Compositions into which we enter full of expectations that do not always correspond with what we see. And out of which we step back into reality, an eternity – or some ten minutes – later.

LA RAISON DES OMBRES

2015

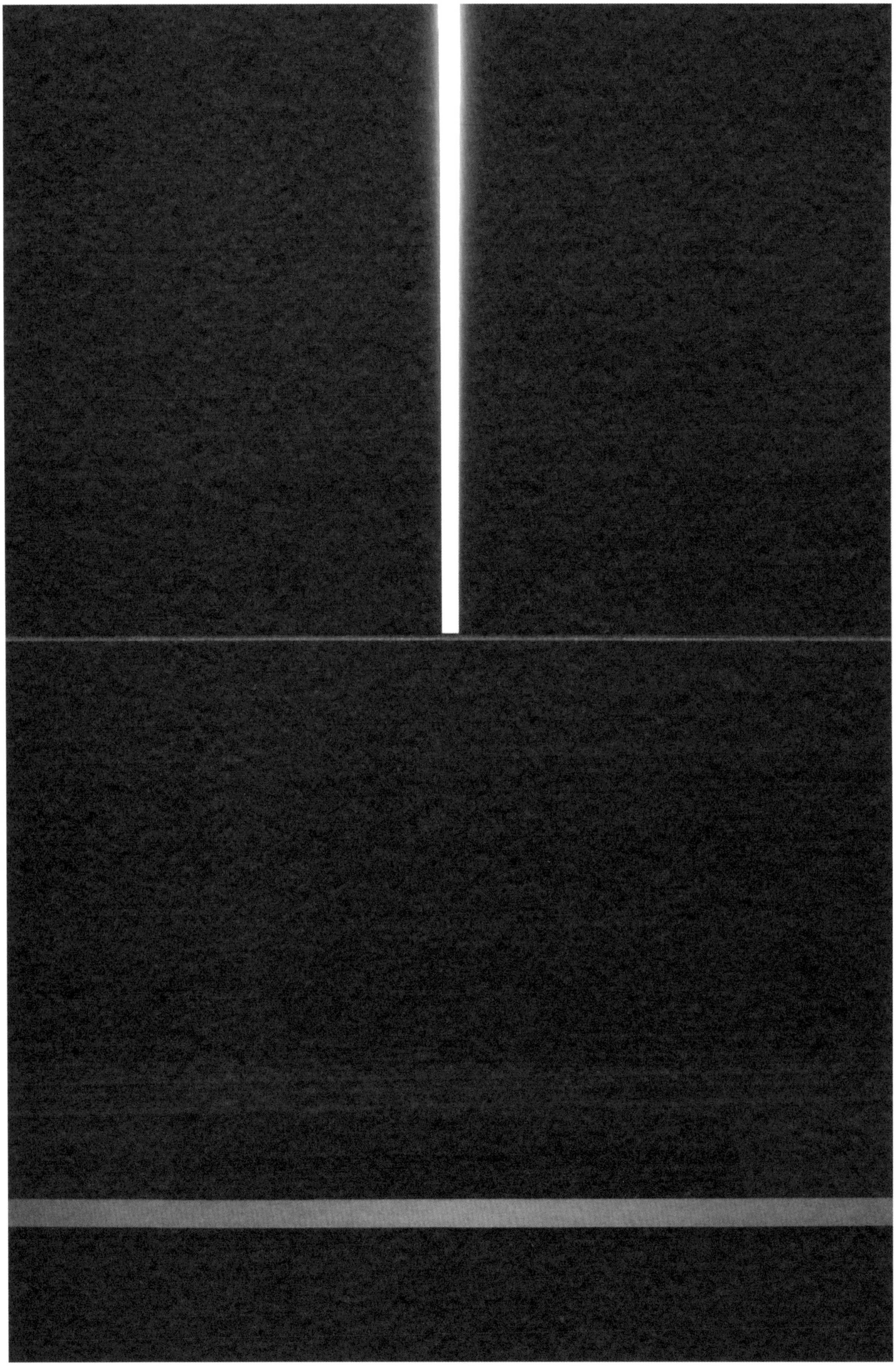

NOTHING IS MORE VISIBLE THAN THINGS HIDDEN

2019

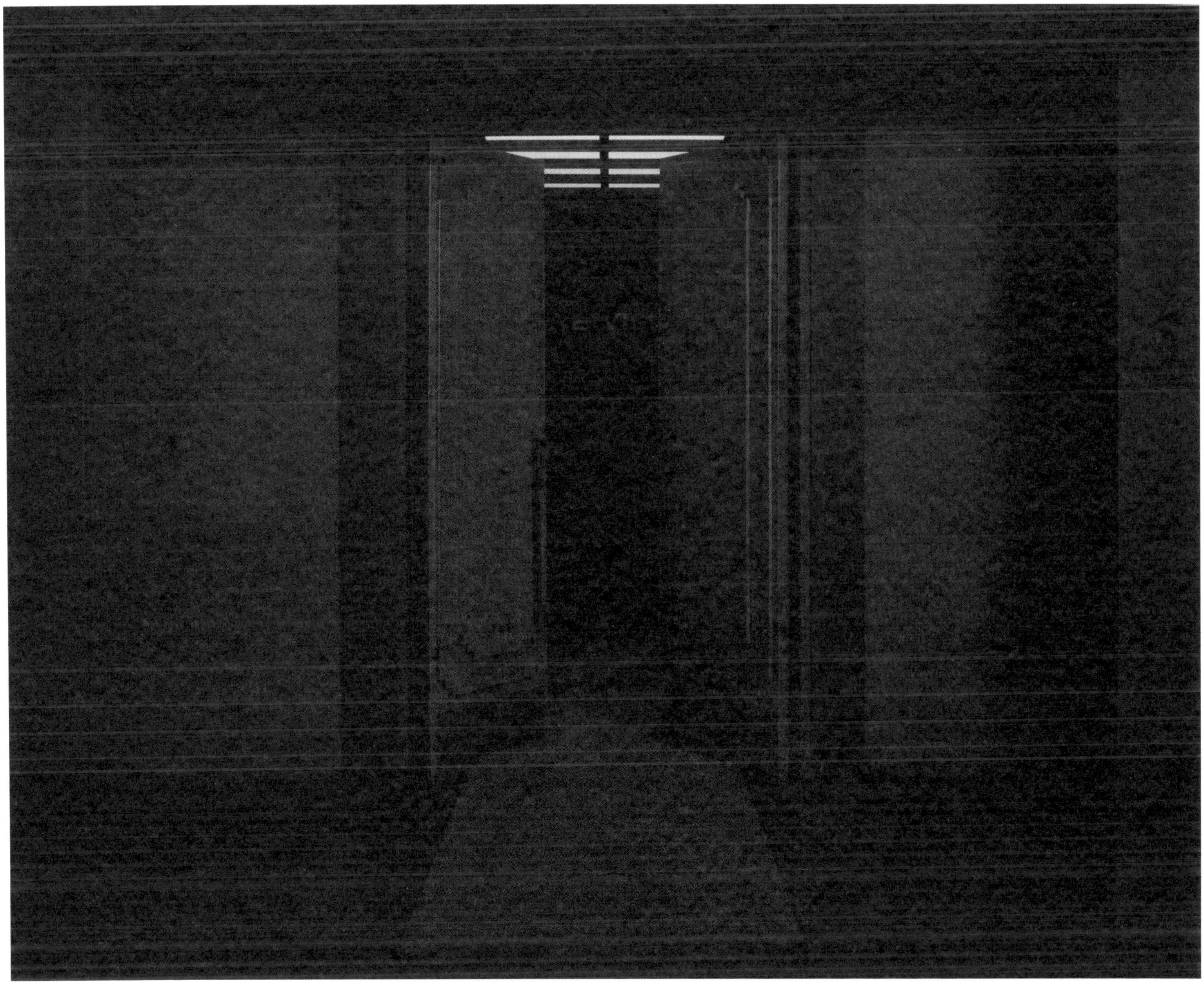

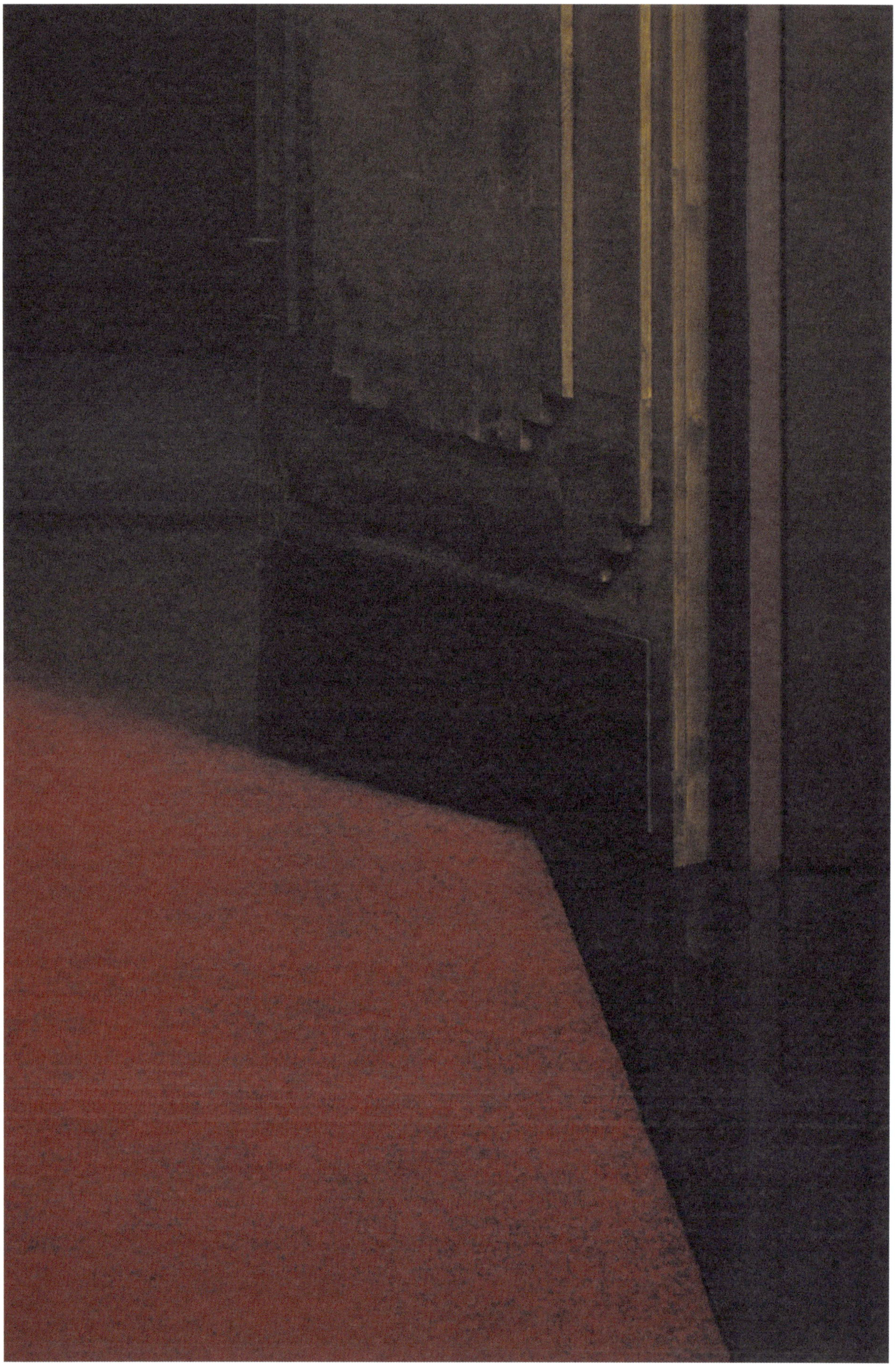

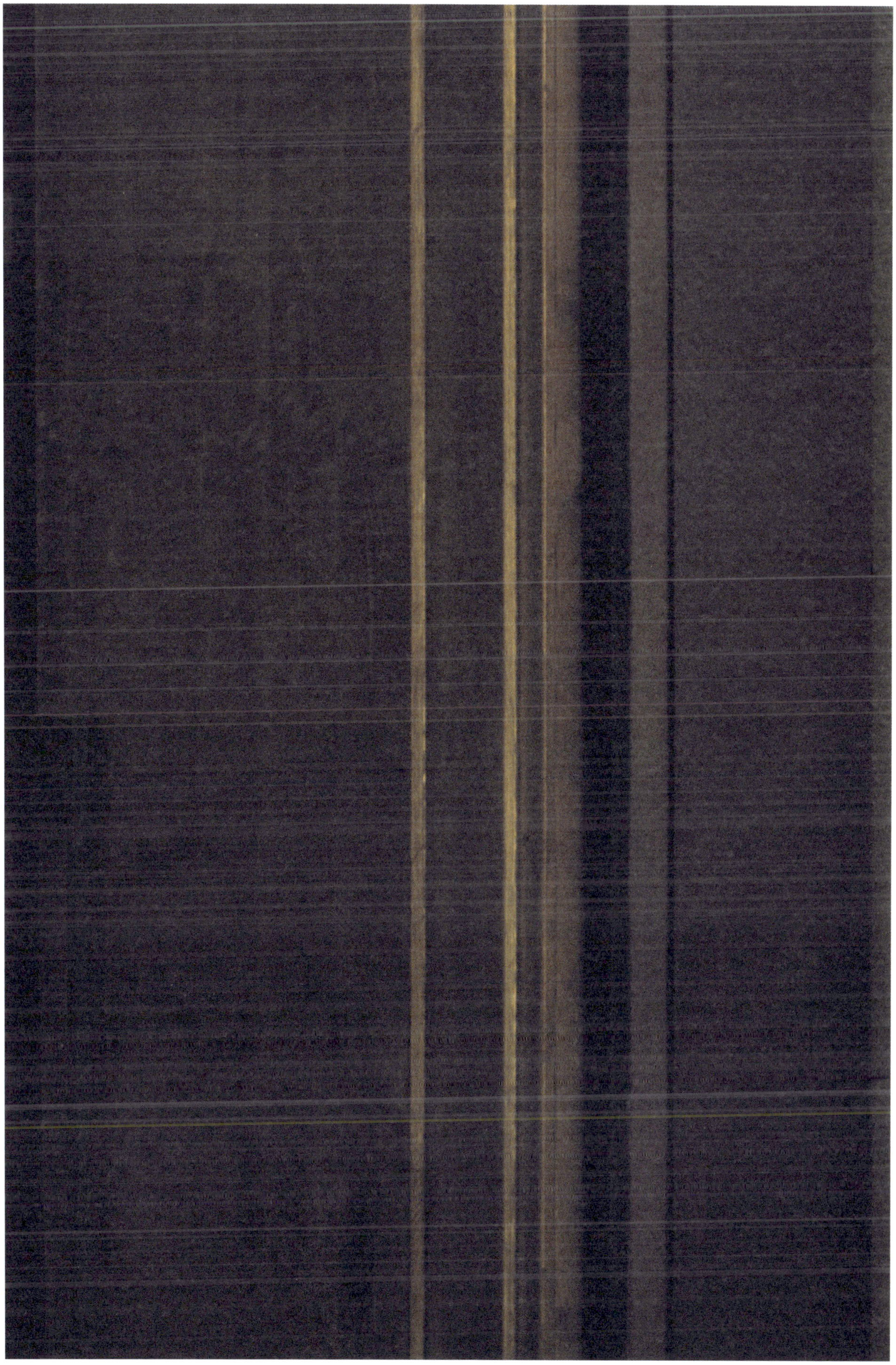

LA RAISON DES MIROIRS

2020-2023

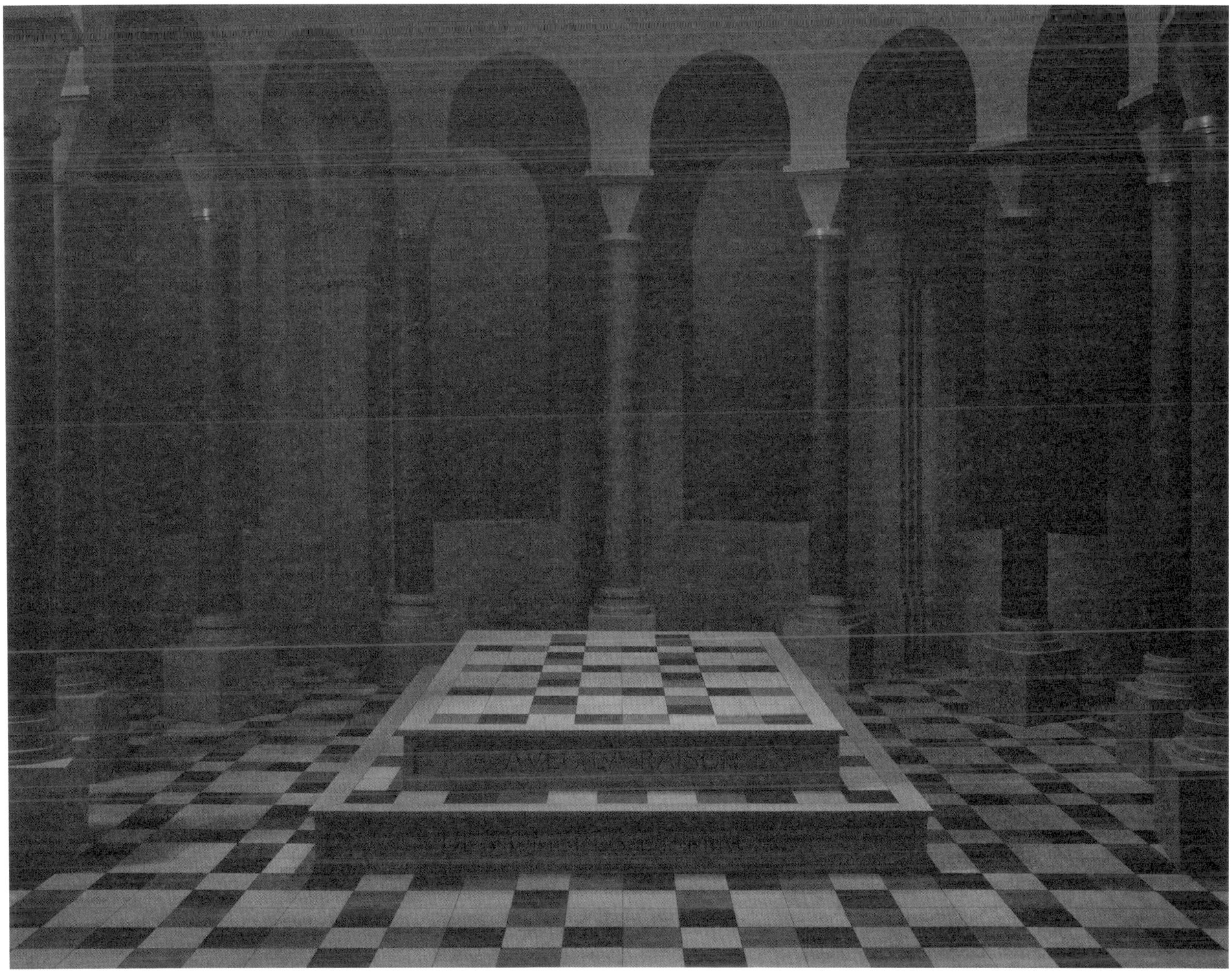
AVEC LA RAISON

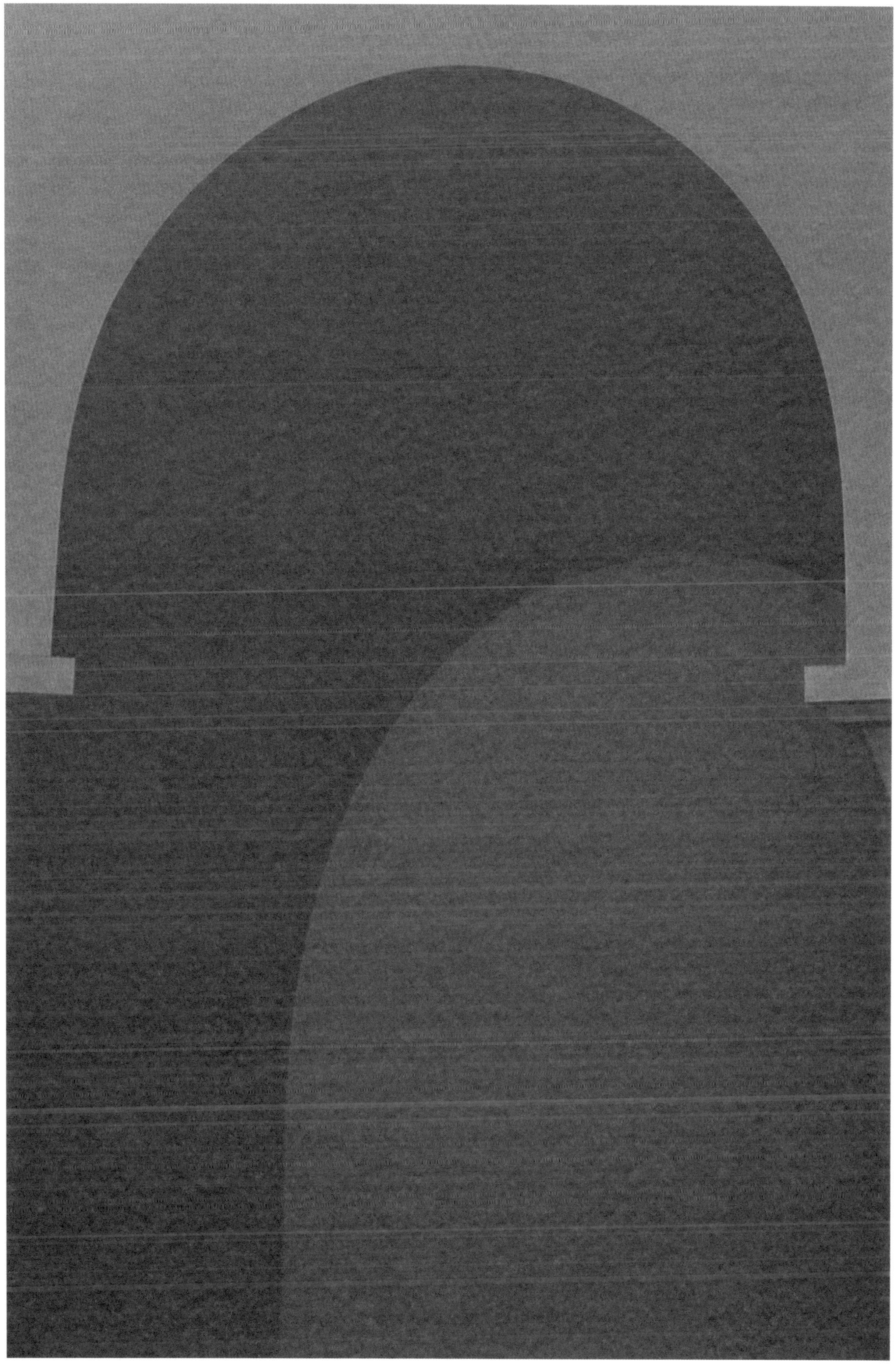

Des ombres et miroirs I

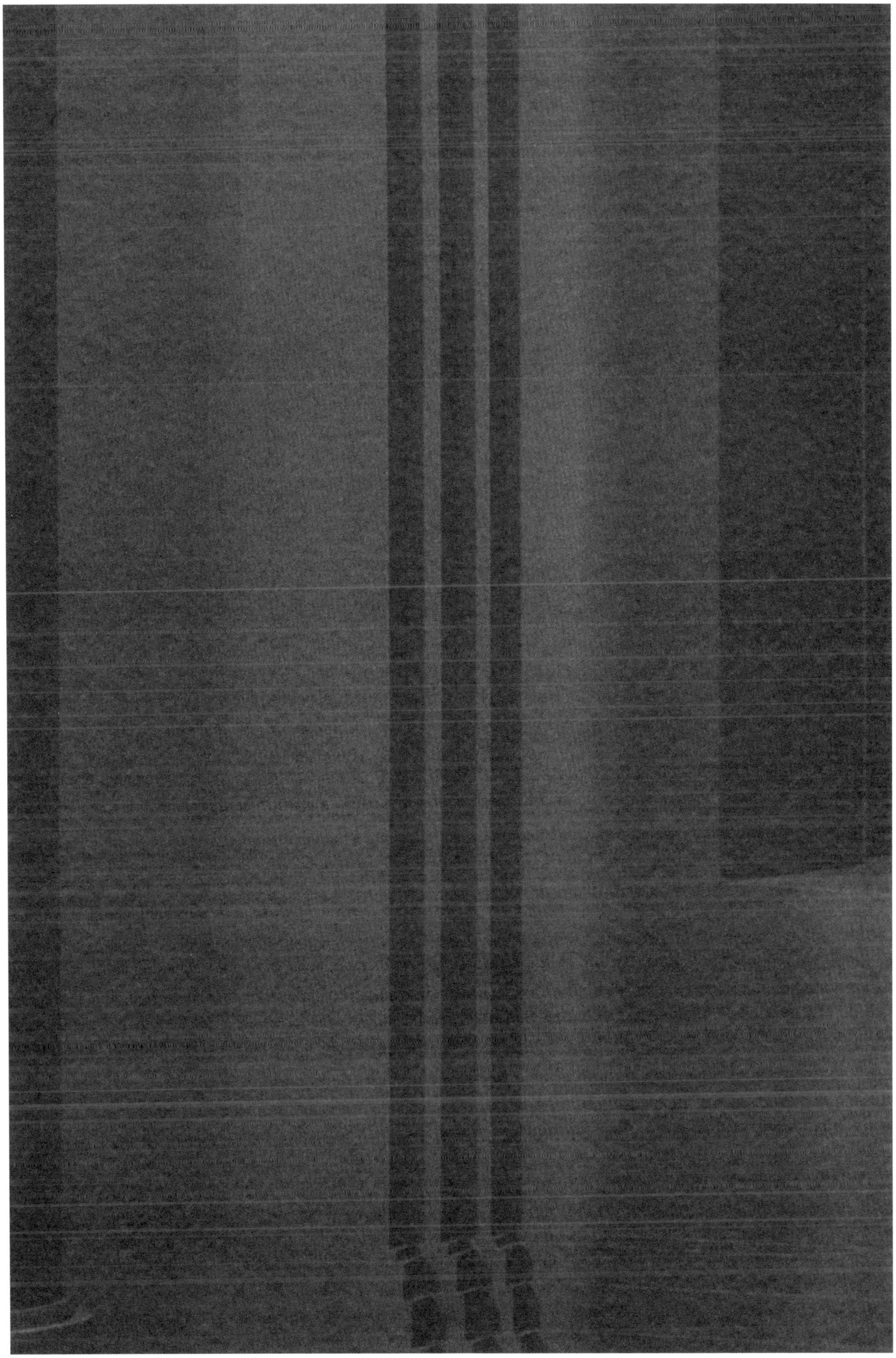

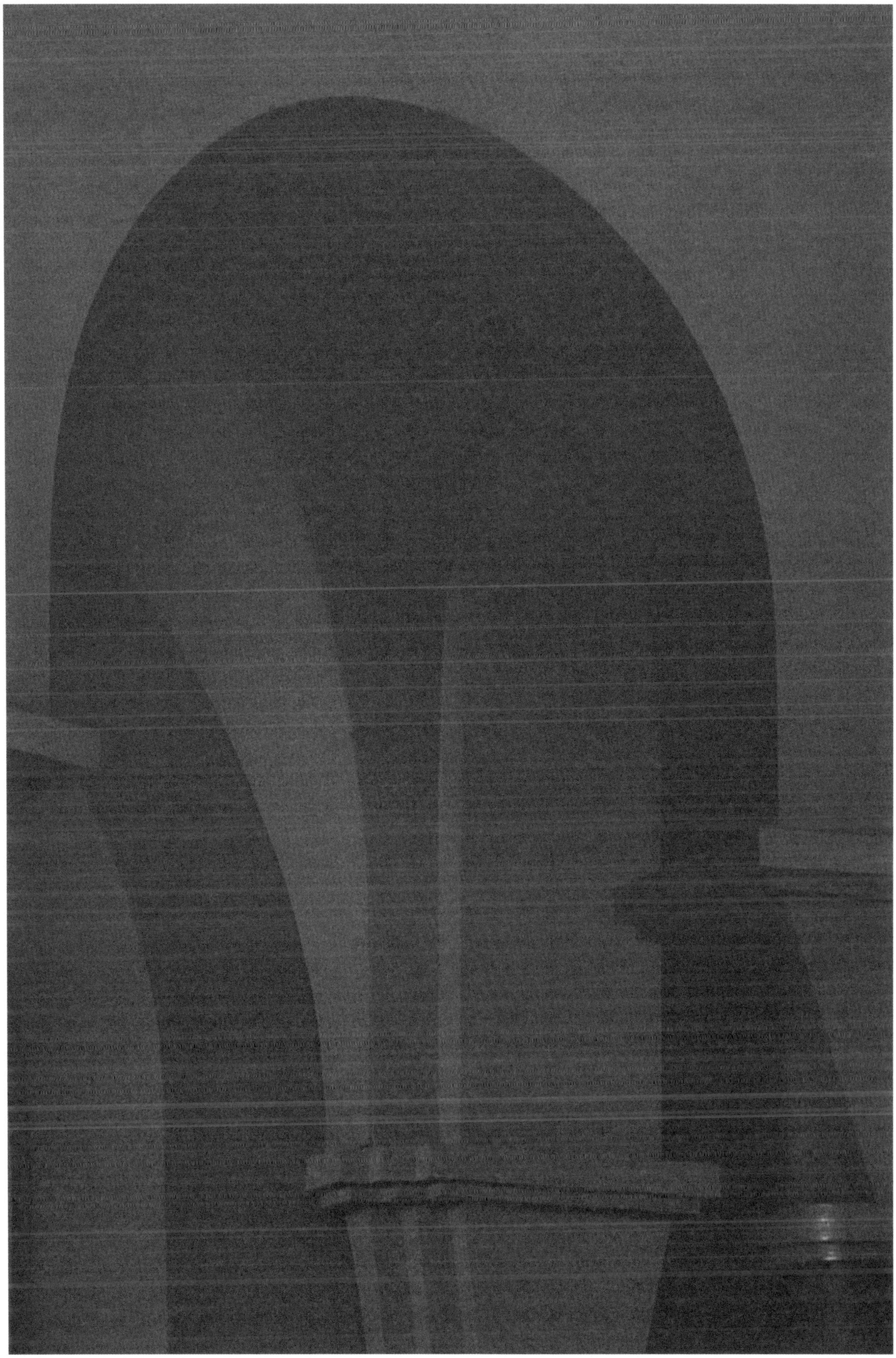

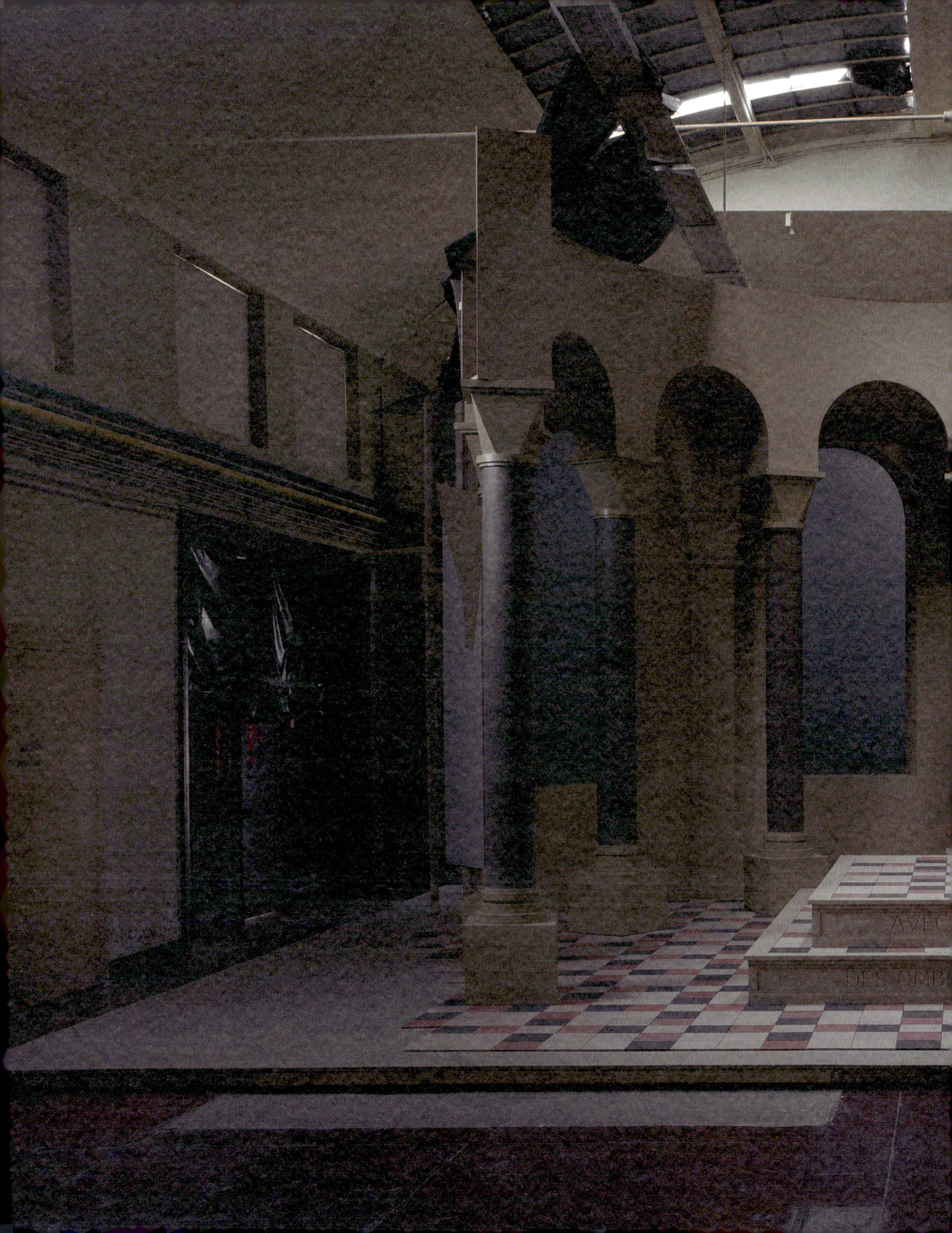
AVEC
DES OMB

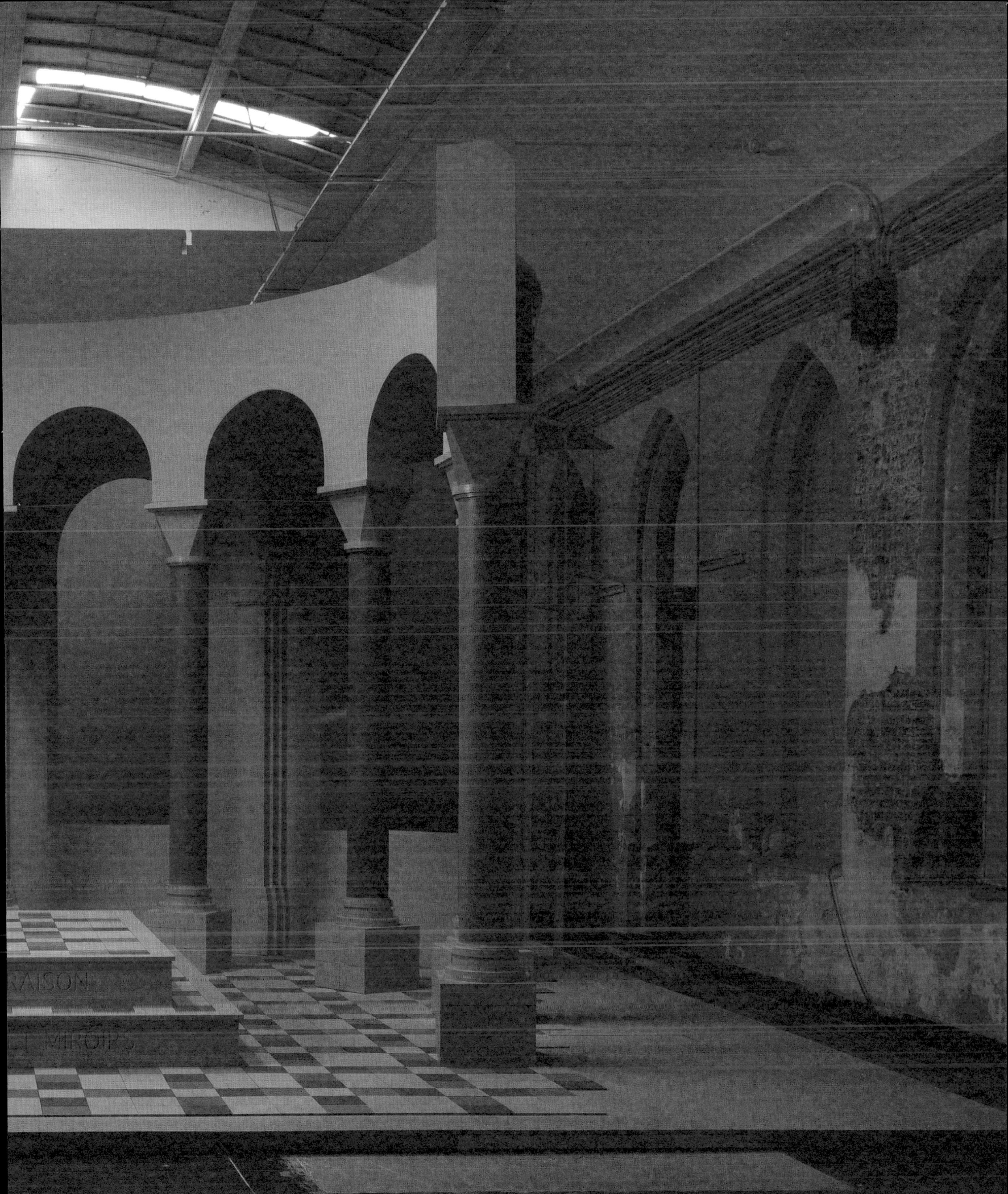
RAISON
MIROIRS

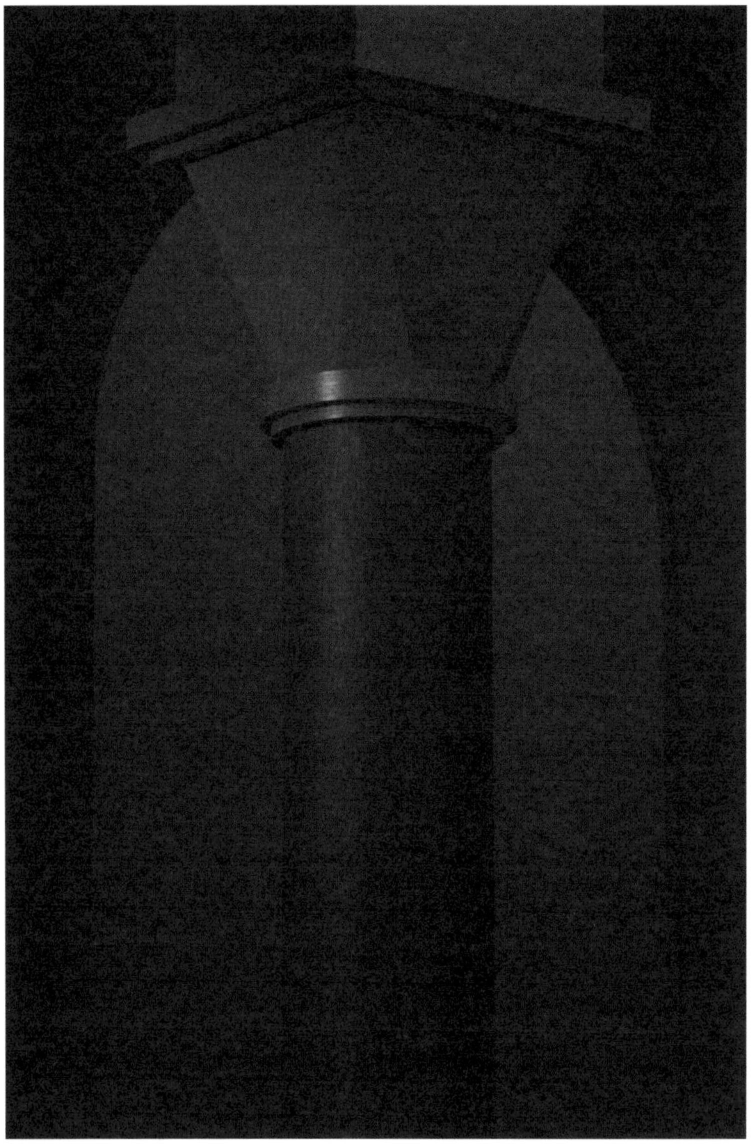

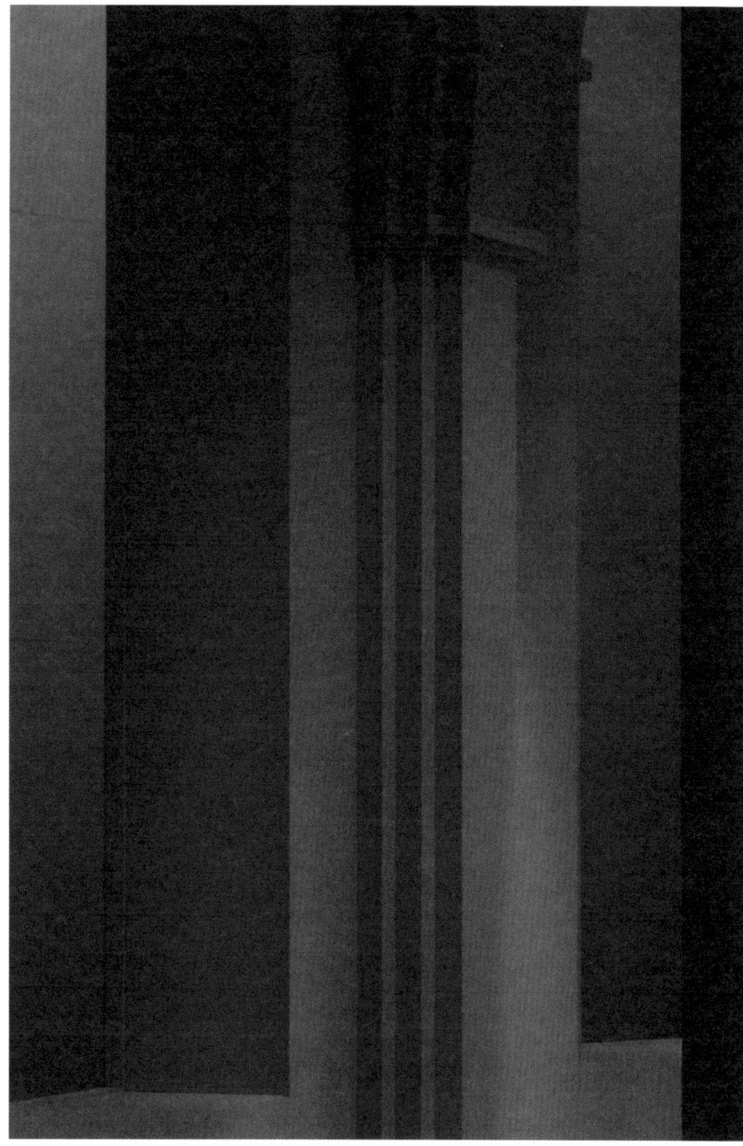

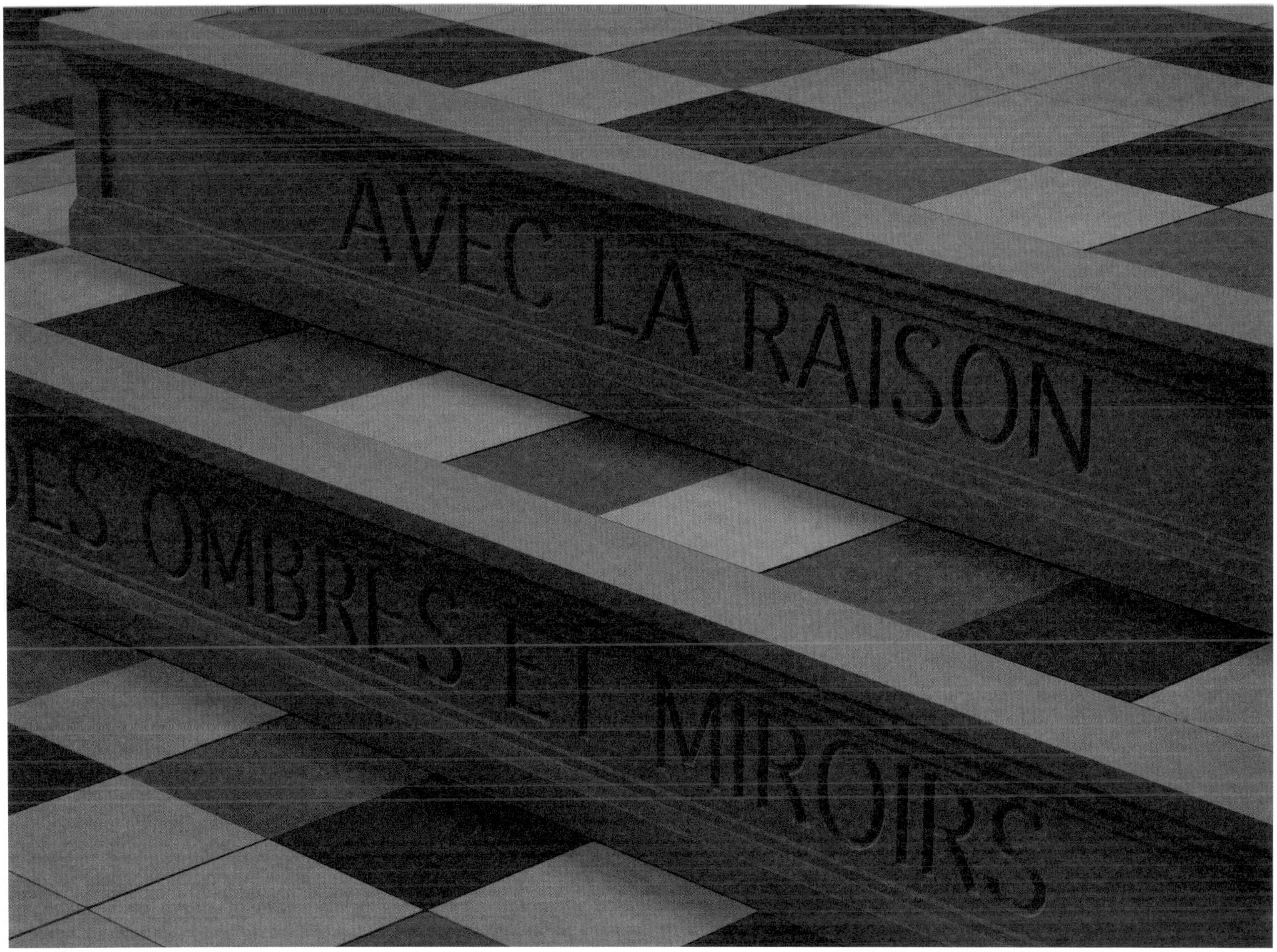
AVEC LA RAISON
DES OMBRES ET MIROIRS

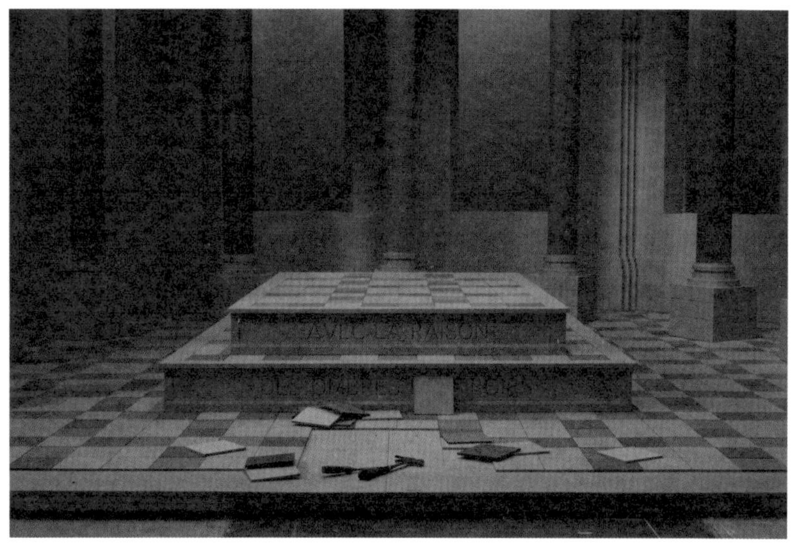

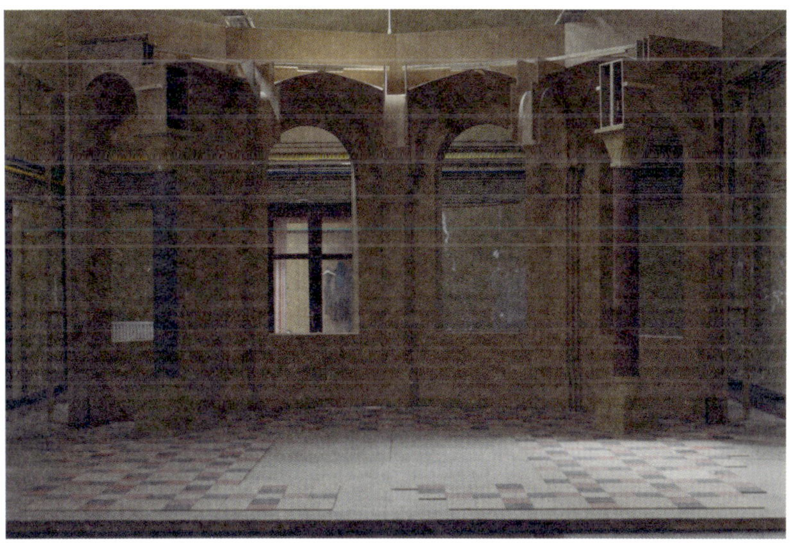

AT THE BREAK OF DAY

2023

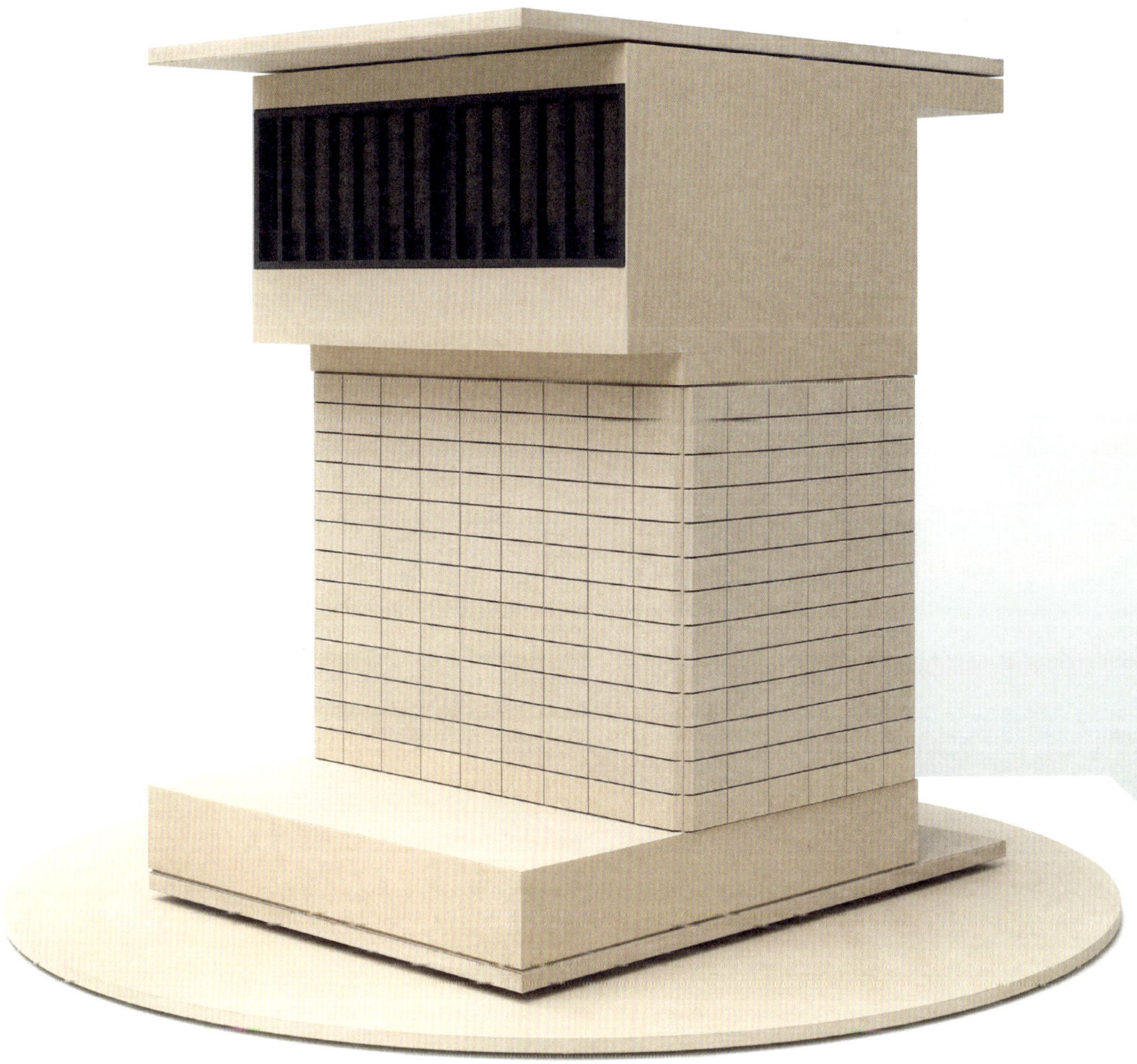

Study

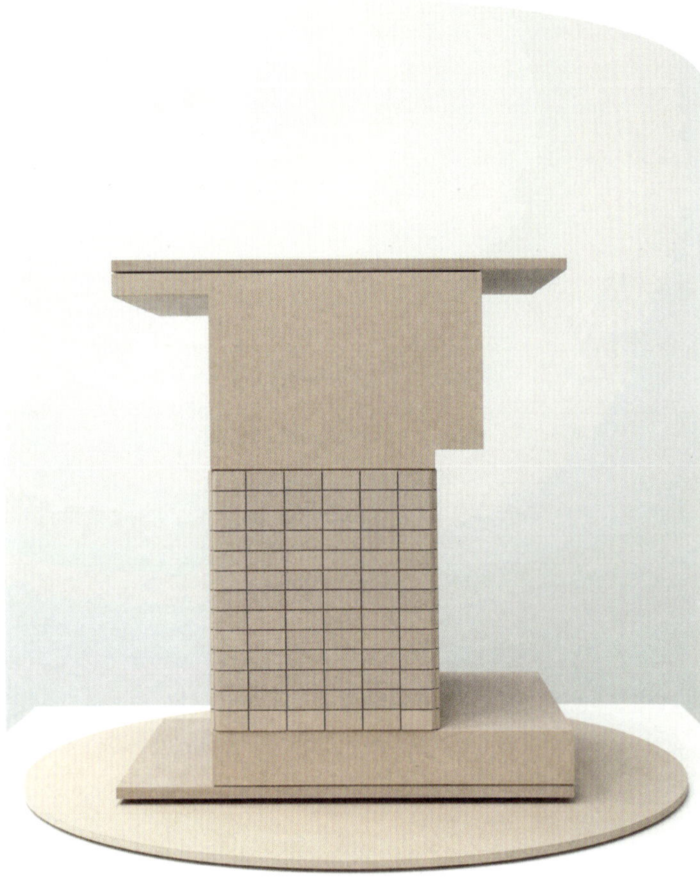
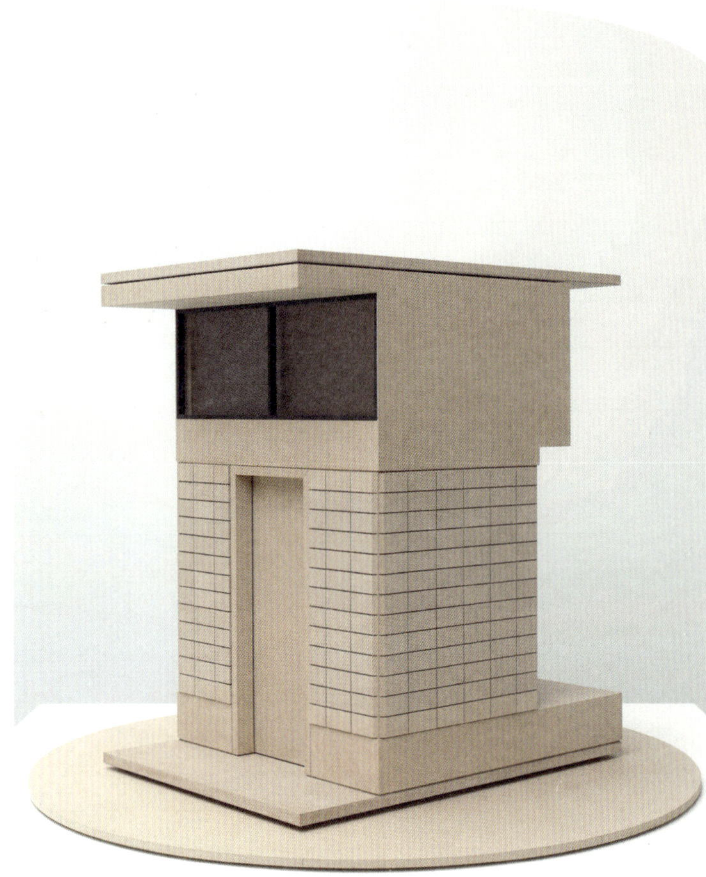
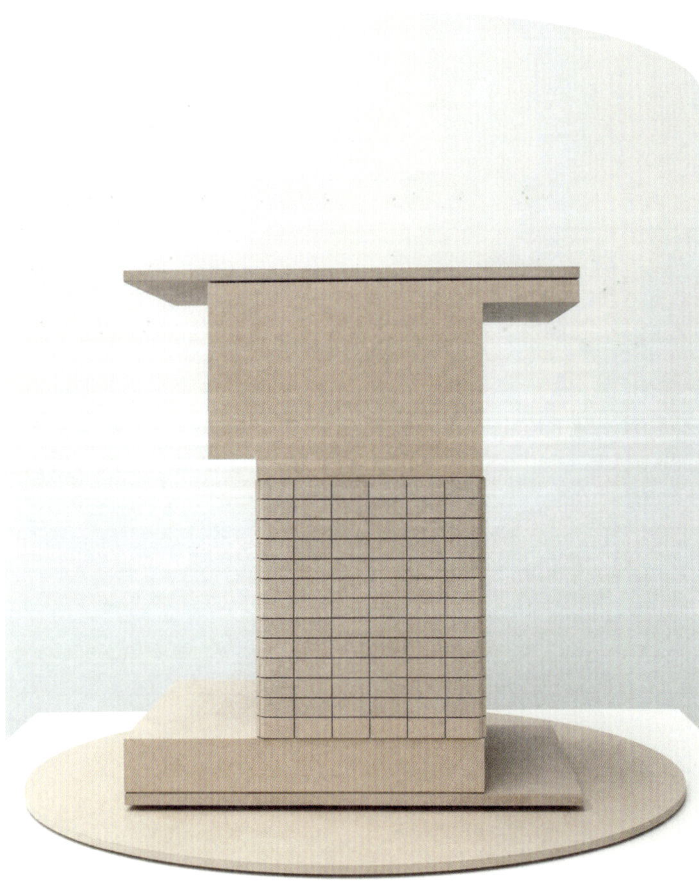
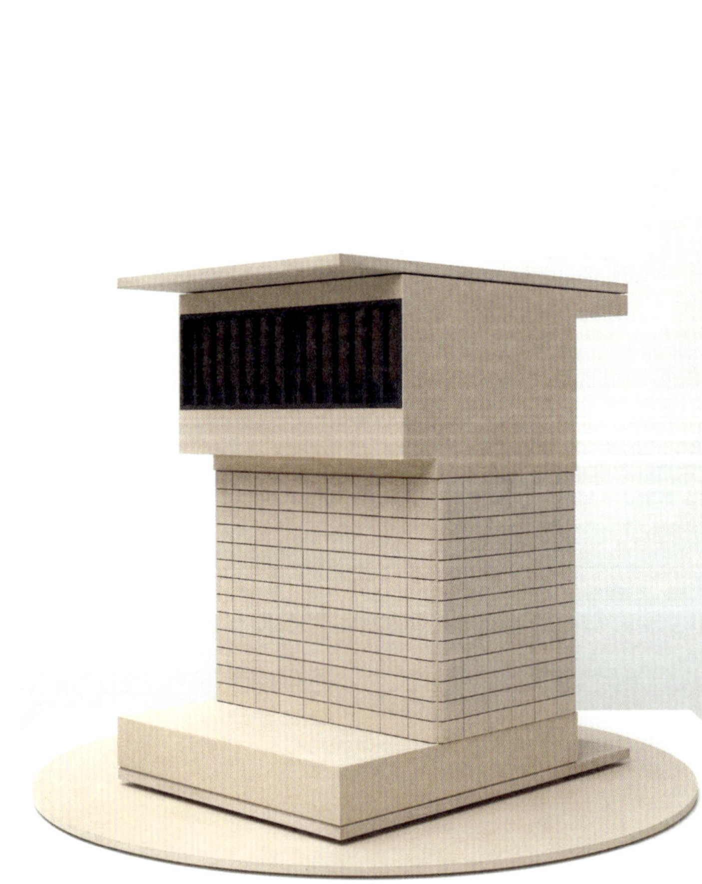

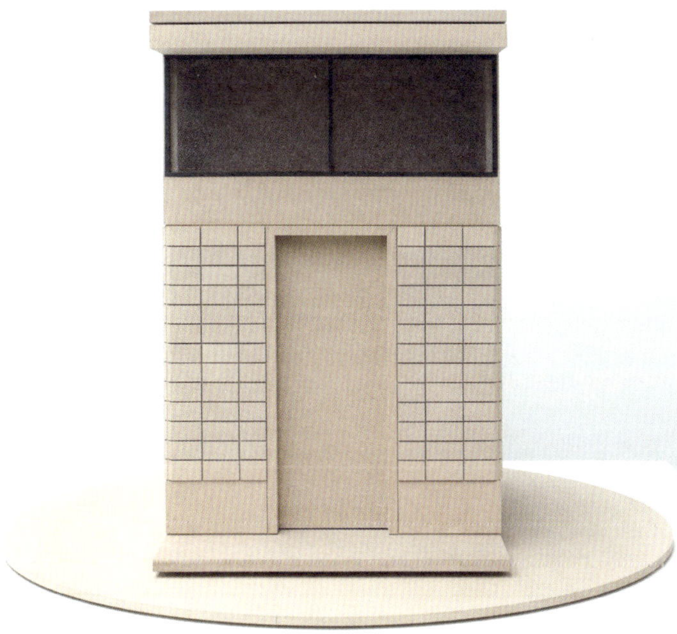
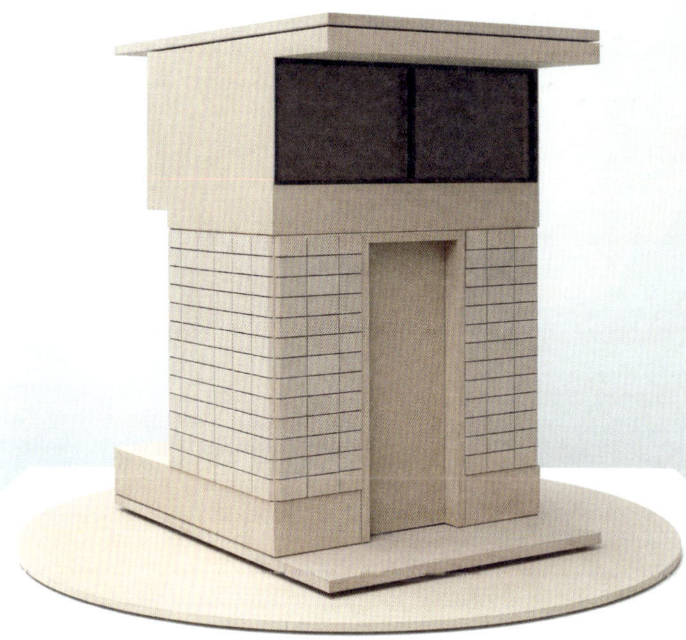
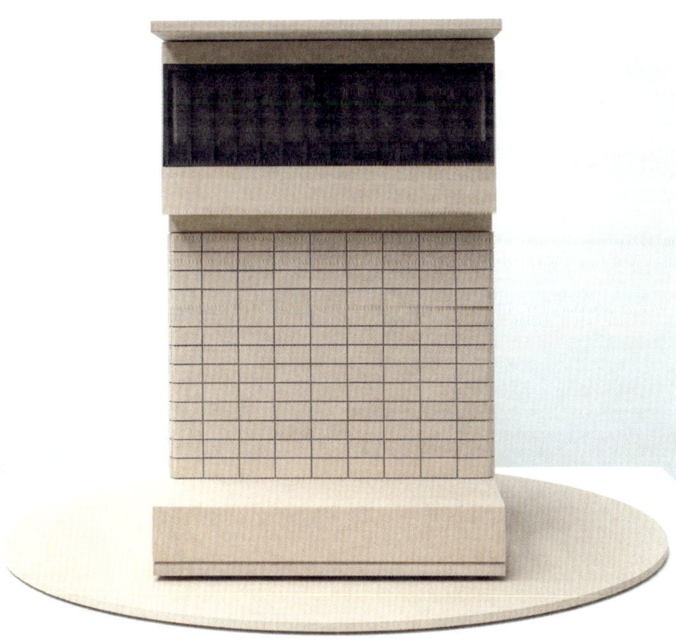
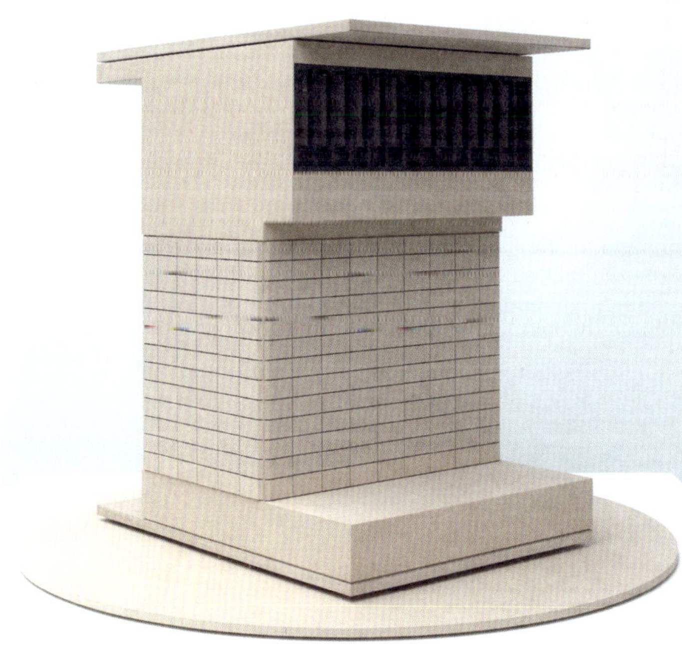

NONE WHATSOEVER

2023

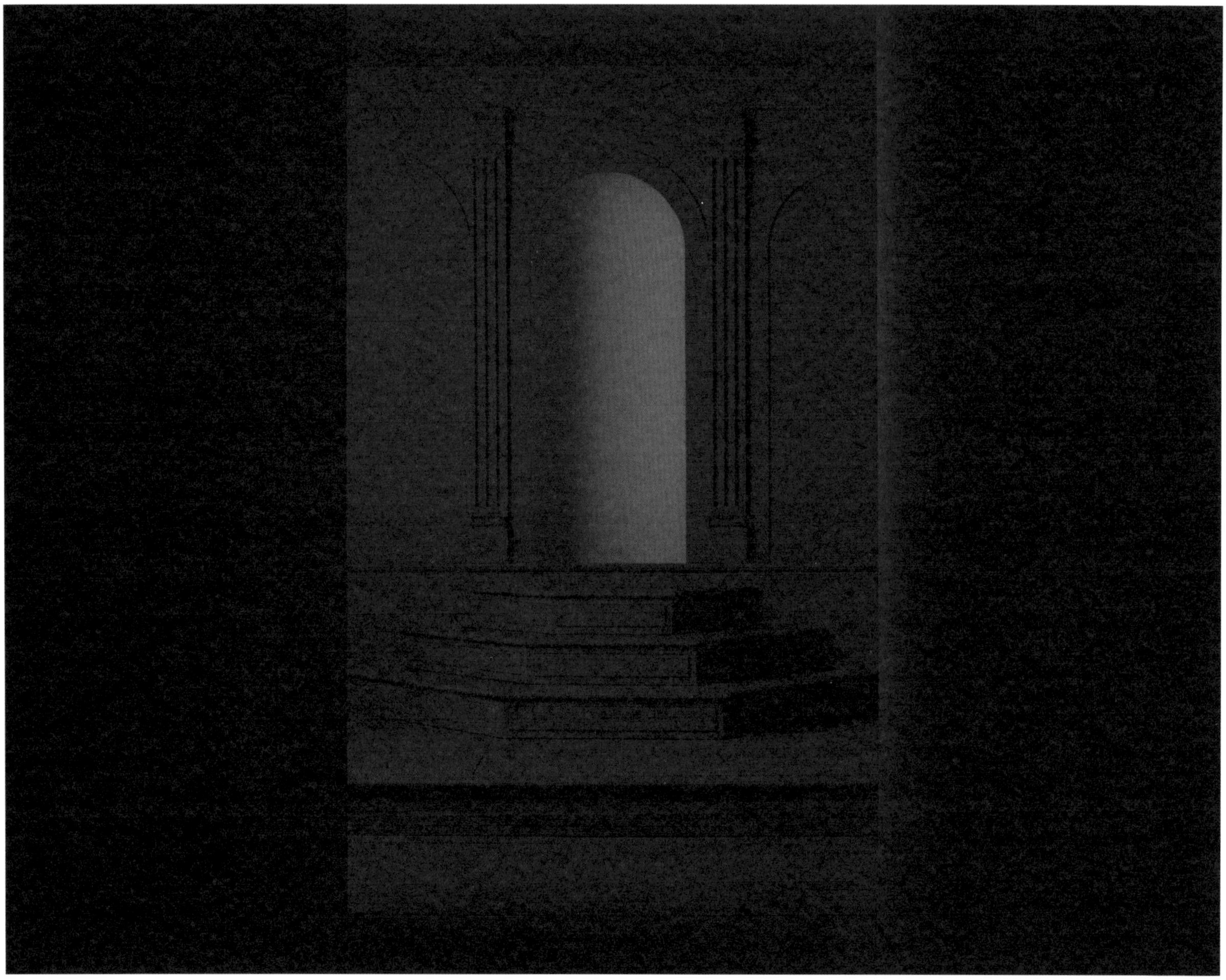

Lefere's methodological approach bears some resemblance to scientific research. In fact, he frequently collaborates with scientists in his work. The series 'Shadow is a hole' arose from a long-term collaboration with Dr. Martin Smith, professor of forensic and biological anthropology at Bournemouth University. Smith's work includes excavations of neolithic sites in Great Britain. These early traces of human existence left in the landscape fascinate Lefere. He photographs these sites, albeit in his own particular way. The photos are always taken at the very last light of day or using the flash. Shrouded in shadows, the sites appear to have had their mystical character returned to them by Lefere, as if in apology for their exposure by the archaeological activities. This series shows Lefere's profound affinity for archaeology. Just like an archaeologist, he carefully and slowly reveals significance in what previously lay hidden.

FORENSIC SERIES

ALL MODELS ARE WRONG; SOME MODELS ARE USEFUL

by Martin Smith

The power of simulation in scientific research and teaching

As someone working in the sciences it would be easy to conceive of oneself, and also to be regarded by others, as a hard-headed, cold-hearted, logical positivist, with a pronounced lack of romance in their soul. In regard to my work at least, there is hopefully some truth in such a view, as otherwise I would be unlikely to perform well in my job. As scientists, our work must be firmly rooted in verifiable evidence and rests entirely on what we can observe, measure and substantiate, as opposed to the comparative freedom that might be ascribed to artists, who are at liberty to imagine anything they wish. My subject involves the analysis and interpretation of evidence obtained from human remains deriving mostly from archaeological settings. In most cases this involves preserved bones and teeth, although in some instances we are further fortunate in having the opportunity to learn from other body tissues as well in the form of mummified remains.

In undertaking research into the human past we are attempting to inquire about the nature of events that are often no longer directly observable. To be able to say anything about past events requires us to accept the 'uniformitarian principle'. This is simply to say that we must start from the assumption that the natural laws and processes we can observe now, have always worked in the same way, and also that the patterns of material evidence left by current actions will mirror those that would have been produced by the same actions in the past. If this basic premise is correct (and we have no reason to think that it is not) this places us in a position where we can investigate the past through simulation – i.e. by undertaking experiments to establish whether the material signature of a given event or process is consistent with a particular form of evidence preserved in the archaeological record or at a scene of forensic investigation. In designing experiments that simulate a particular event or set of conditions, it is always the case that only a portion of relevant conditions will be somewhere close to correct. All simulations are flawed by nature as human design can only ever exert control over a limited range of aspects in 'recreating' a given event. It is therefore the case that all such experimentation entails acknowledgement of the shortcomings of models as inherently imperfect imitations that will always fall short of reality. At the same time good experimental design, focusing on the most important aspects under investigation can produce results that help address questions which often cannot be tested by other means. In this sense the commonly cited axiom that "all models are wrong, but some models are useful" underlines the extent to which one of the greatest strengths of the scientific approach is in fact its willingness to accept imprecision in the pursuit of accuracy.

Simulations as Research Tools:

Some work I have undertaken in recent years that involved the creation of simulations in order to answer research questions began with questions raised as to whether particular patterns of damage seen in preserved archaeological skulls were signs

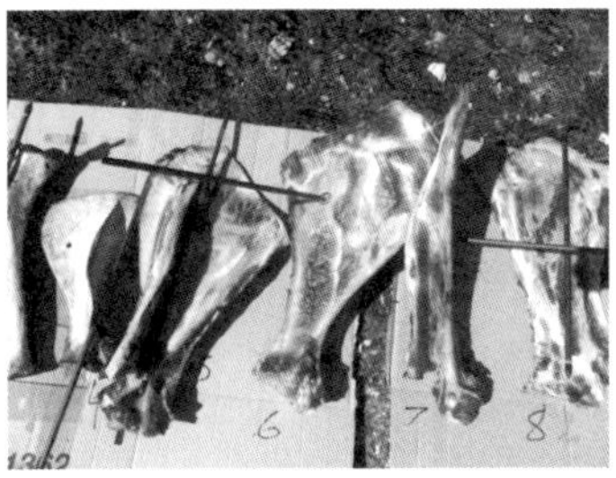

I

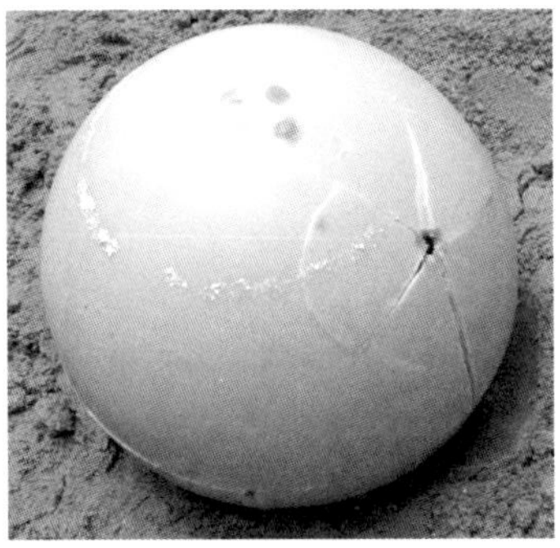

II

I Experimental samples in the form of cattle scapulae (shoulder blades) shot with bolts from a crossbow. These large flat areas of bone go some way towards simulating plates of bone in the human skeleton including the pelvis or skull.

II A Polyurethane (brittle plastic) sphere used to simulate the human skull in experiments investigating ballistic injuries. The sphere is filled with gelatin to simulate the soft tissues inside the skull. The fracture pattern around the bullet entry point is a distinctive form known as a stellate fracture that is characteristically seen in gunshot wounds to the head.

of past violence as opposed to having been produced by some more mundane cause, such as the respective bones being damaged accidentally when the excavators recovered them. This interest initially grew from examining the remains of Neolithic people, from the time of the first farmers dating from around 3,600 BC. Contrary to the view we had of this period a generation ago, it now seems, on the basis of careful study of human bones that this was a stressed and challenging time, when conflict between communities was frequent and where trespassing into the wrong territory could cost someone their life. In particular, I was interested to know whether elliptical holes penetrating some Neolithic skulls could in fact have been caused by stone weapons. This was resolved through shooting flint tipped arrows at the scapulae (shoulder blades) of cattle and pigs, with the results resembling the defects in the human skulls very closely[I].

Whilst these experiments were effective in answering this specific question, similar queries persisted regarding the effects of more powerful projectile weapons such as crossbows and pre-modern firearms in causing head injuries. These latter queries could not be answered by simply shooting at flat pieces of animal bone as the nature of the head as a dynamic, closed 'sphere' containing liquid and soft tissues means that such powerful impacts have more complex effects and produce patterns of injury to bone involving distinctive fracture patterns, rather than simple holes in the skull.
An obvious solution might be to use skulls or rather heads (with skin, brains etc.) as experimental samples. But of course, such a choice would bring obvious ethical problems – I would certainly have no wish to use donated human cadavers for example, whilst other mammal species have heads that are very different from our own due to the large size of the human brain and so the results would be invalid. In looking for an alternative I came across a synthetic bone material made of brittle polyurethane plastic that was developed specifically as having similar properties to human bone for use in training orthopaedic surgeons[II]. The same material was also available as hollow spheres, representing the cranium, which my students and I were able to make use of by filling the spheres with ballistic gelatine (constituted to the same density as human soft tissue) to mimic the contents of the skull. These simple and imperfect simulations in fact worked very well in reproducing the kinds of fracture seen in modern gunshot wounds, with various results that were specific to the crossbow and black powder musket we used in these investigations.

Other simulations I have conducted with my research students have involved similarly spectacular arrangements such as the re-creation of Roman style funeral pyres and accidental modern house fires. These latter have used whole deer carcasses (culled due to over-population and not killed for the experiments) as proxies for humans in order to investigate the extent to which patterns of burning in the recovered bones differed and so could indicate whether a body was burned deliberately as opposed to being that of an accidental fire victim.

A third kind of simulation I have been involved in over recent years is of a virtual nature. It was realised in the 19th century that comparative measurements taken from offset photographs of the same object or landscape could be used to mathematically calculate the shape of the subject in the images. This application has undergone a great degree of development over the following centuries and has now matured as digital photogrammetry. This technique involves the comparison of multiple photographs taken at differing angles in order to generate a three-dimensional model

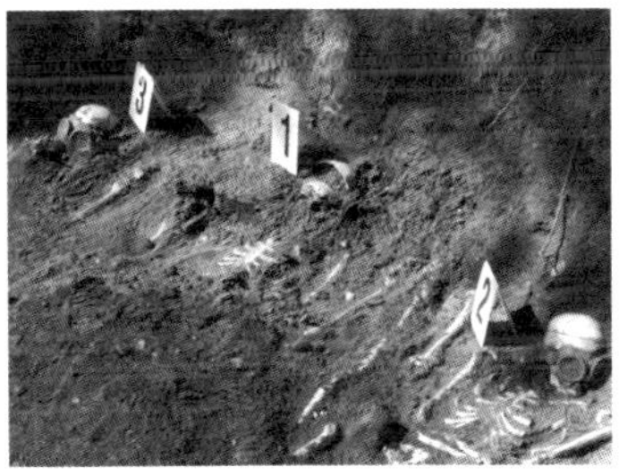

III

of the object in view. The process involves a high degree of computer processing power but can produce impressive results, where complex objects can be captured as virtual replicas. The human skeleton presents a variety of complex three-dimensional forms which have always presented a problem in terms of recording. Two dimensional photographs and drawings have strengths of their own, but are also limited in terms of the information they can convey. The human skull in particular is a highly complex three-dimensional structure that is difficult to represent even using multiple views from differing angles. Moreover, photographic representations can suffer from distortions of perspective which are made worse when close up views are used to try and show greater detail. The option to create highly detailed virtual copies of parts of the skeleton offers exciting possibilities, both in terms of providing a new and more versatile form of permanent record for cases when such remains are later reburied, and also for being able to share such 3D 'virtual' simulations easily with others. Student projects I have supervised applying this technique have ranged in size from the documentation of mass graves (again simulated for research purposes), to the recreation of skulls to check measurements against the originals, to the detailed recording of sword cuts in the bones of a group of 10th century Vikings, buried together in a former Roman quarry pit, apparently after a raiding party had fallen foul of the locals.

Simulations as Teaching Exercises:

The ultimate aim of teaching is to produce competent, versatile individuals with a range of skills that position them well to commence a career in their chosen field. Engaging in practical activities as part of a course of structured learning allows students to make connections and build aptitudes in ways that are seldom achievable simply through reading or being told how to do things. In this sense our subject is often at a disadvantage, as the events we wish our students to experience cannot simply be created or accessed to order. The excavation of human remains from archaeological sites is a frequent occurrence in itself, that can form a useful aspect of student training, but remains a type of evidence that cannot easily be predicted or planned in advance, nor can we guarantee a burial for every student to excavate. More complex arrangements of such remains as encountered in scenarios of natural disasters or the investigation of modern conflicts and genocide require further specialist skills to investigate. However, these latter present even greater challenges to an instructor wishing to provide realistic and relevant training experiences. An aspect common to both archaeological and forensic investigations is that these are unrepeatable exercises. A buried body or skeleton cannot be excavated twice, once bones or artefacts have been removed, the spatial relationships between them no longer exist, whilst a court will not permit a witness to go back and present the same evidence a second time. This presents a problem in that for such crucial exercises the notion of 'learning on the job' and 'picking it up as one goes along' is simply not an option.

As the above occurrences are impossible to predict or arrange in advance, an alternative is to create simulations of these phenomena, allowing students to experience them in a form that is both sufficiently realistic to be useful, but also safe, both for participants and the 'evidence' they are set to investigate. For our forensic archaeology students, who are studying to acquire the skills needed to locate and recover modern buried remains, we therefore spend time each winter digging 'graves' into which plastic, replica skeletons, normally used in anatomical teaching are placed, complete with clothes,

III Replica skeletons appearing from the ground during excavation by Bournemouth University students.

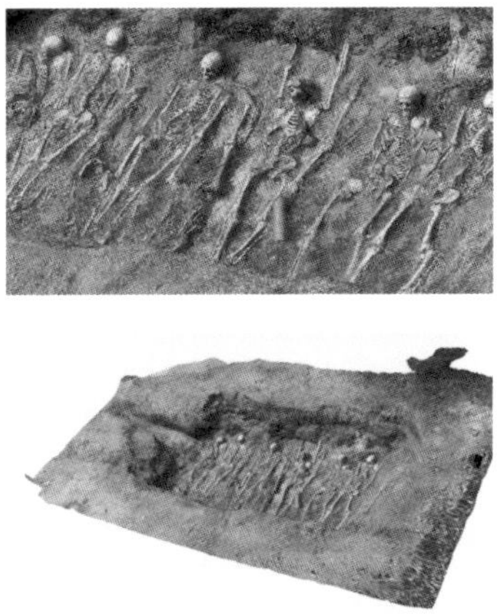

IV

personal items and objects that might assist with dating the 'crime'[III]. These arrangements serve to simulate shallow burials following a murder, with the students then working in teams first to locate the graves (months later when the vegetation has regrown) and then to excavate them systematically, producing drawings, photographs and written records at a standard submissible to a court. A further team exercise executed on a larger scale replicates the kind of mass graves that are a feature of the modern world in too many regions affected by conflict, genocide and human rights violations[IV]. Again, replica skeletons are buried, furnished with clothing and personal effects. Once placed and ready for the grave to be backfilled, the visual effect of this imitation arrangement is in fact very considerable. On one occasion the exercise was visited by a photographer who had worked for the United Nations in documenting mass graves relating to war crimes in the former Yugoslavia. He was quite struck by just how closely the simulation resembled real examples of such graves and commented that the greatest difference was simply that the simulation lacked the odours associated with the real thing. During this exercise the emphasis is on replicating the working circumstances for a team challenged with such a task, requiring considerable physical labour, leadership, specialised job roles (excavator, photographer, surveyor and others) and a high degree of collaborative team working. These recovery exercises are followed by an assessment of a different skill set in which students present the 'evidence' they have gathered in a simulated courtroom. The most striking feature of the latter for us as staff has always been the extent to which this scenario exerts a strong psychological effect on the participants, who often find the courtroom assessment to be a nerve wracking experience, despite being fully conscious that it is only a simulation. The situation is fictitious, yet the reactions are entirely real.

Spanning the Great Divide: seeing what isn't there

Returning to the wider field of biological anthropology (the study of human populations over time), aspects of the subject that focus upon excavated human skeletons are constrained by a range of perennial challenges. Rather than examining single skeletons, we more frequently arrive at conclusions about past life through studying populations. Such investigations therefore principally focus on cemeteries rather than individuals. The remains of past people that are accessible to us are frequently broken and fragmented, and subject to a range of processes that have hindered their preservation in the ground. However, not only are individual skeletons often incomplete, but also the wider groupings in which they were buried are often only partially represented by the remains recovered through excavation. Such excavations can only access the bones of people who were buried in a given location rather than never buried or interred elsewhere. Nor can they retrieve bones that were simply not preserved by the local soils, those that have been destroyed by previous building or quarrying etc., or those that simply lie beyond the limits of the area being excavated. When the results of a cemetery excavation are published, the authors are therefore in fact presenting only a 'sample, of a sample of a sample' (etc.) from which conclusions are drawn regarding the wider population that lived in a given region and period. It is an inherent characteristic of the field that we strive to produce the fullest picture, with the greatest resolution that we can achieve from only a fraction of what was once present.

Photography is by definition a selective endeavour that presents the viewer with a sample of visual information, chosen from an infinitely wider set of possibilities. In this

IV Still image of a three-dimensional virtual (computer) model of a simulated mass grave. This model was produced by combining multiple overlapping images taken at differing angles.

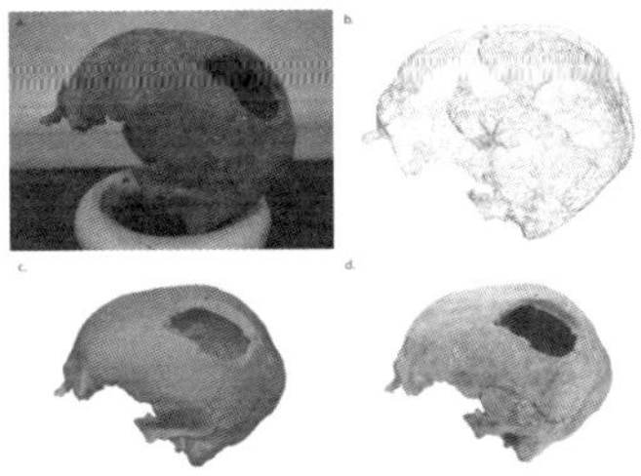

V

sense photographic art is always as much about what is not in the image as what is. Our eye, and by extension our mind is taken beyond the frame of the picture to conceive and ask questions about the wider setting in which the image was produced. In addition to being of explicit value in their own terms, photographic images therefore also hold wider implicit potential in presenting a window onto the wider world in which they were created. This effect is particularly powerful in the case of images of exotic or distant regions that we may never visit, but also with images from the past. Photographs from fifty or a hundred years ago take the viewer into a world which no longer exists, providing a framework onto which we can build a wider mental model of the setting in which the image was originally created. In this sense a photograph offers a sample of information from which a greater whole is then imagined. Sampling, modelling and simulation are intrinsic aspects of the process[V]. In this regard photographic art and scientific inquiry can actually be seen to sit very closely together in conceptual space, rather than being at the opposite ends of a philosophical gulf. The concept underlying archaeological excavation of achieving 'preservation by record' also has strong parallels with approaches in art and especially photography which continually endeavour to capture fleeting and ephemeral aspects of the world which would otherwise be gone.

Whilst their overall objectives might bear more similarity than is obvious at first, the greatest differences between art and science arguably relate to their respective approaches to creating new insights. The scientific method is necessarily constrained by evidence, with a constant tension between imagining what is possible and demonstrating what is not. The commonly cited notion that science can never 'prove' anything, rather only having the power to disprove hypotheses, rests very much on the principle that doubt is healthy whilst casual acceptance is dangerous. By contrast, artists can be seen as enjoying an unfettered ability to create new realities, constrained only by imagination. An example from my own institution came when a colleague from another faculty (Media and Communications) brought his Creative Writing students to study in our human osteology laboratory. Here the lab was used to provide an alternative environment to a standard classroom, whilst some of the remains we care for were used to provide inspiration. Amongst the human remains we curate are 150 skeletons excavated from the cemetery of the former Royal Naval Hospital at Plymouth (in use from 1764 to 1806). On the one hand as anthropologists we subscribe entirely to the view that every skeleton represents the material vestiges of an individual human story. However, we are not at liberty to deviate from the evidence we can verify, as opposed to the students in this instance who were encouraged to start from the same proposition but to each imagine what the 'story' and experiences of one of the Plymouth sailors might have been. Although these approaches differ along both practical and theoretical lines, science and art are not without parallels in a broader sense as both are ultimately concerned with asking questions. In this sense, the default position of science being that 'we do not know' is in fact closely echoed by the creative arts, which continually seek to look at the world in new ways in order to reveal insights that were previously inaccessible rather than simply accepting the dogma of established views. In these senses I have been very privileged to work with Lieven Lefere who I regard very much as a colleague engaged in similar work to my own rather than as coming from the other side of a great divide.

V Stages in the virtual modelling of the preserved skull of a 10th century Viking excavated from a mass grave in Dorset, England; a. one of the initial photographic images, b. 'point cloud' capturing the form of the skull in space, c. 'solid' object created from the point cloud, d. the final model textured using the original images (images: Heather Tamminen).

SKULLS

2016

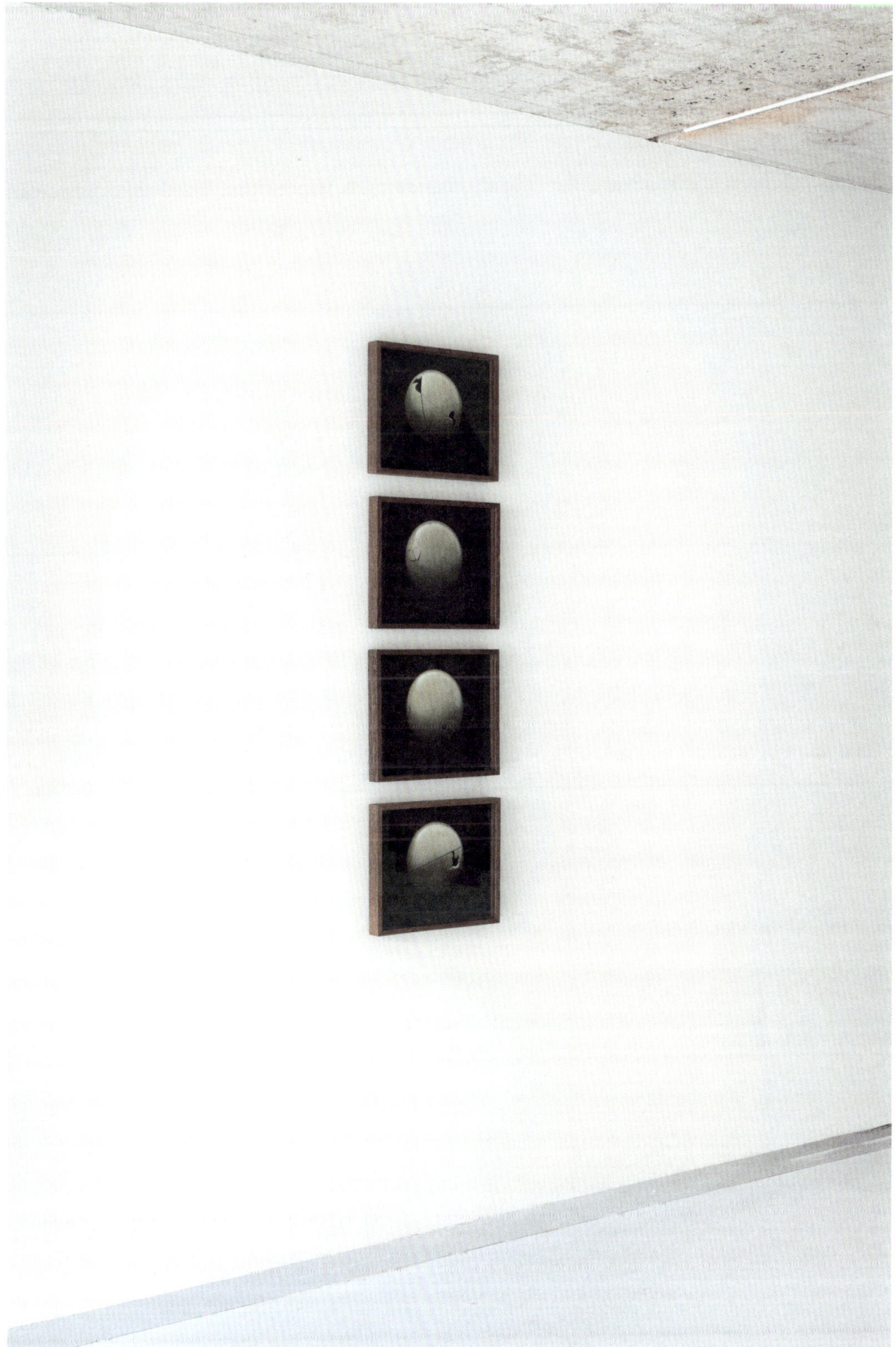

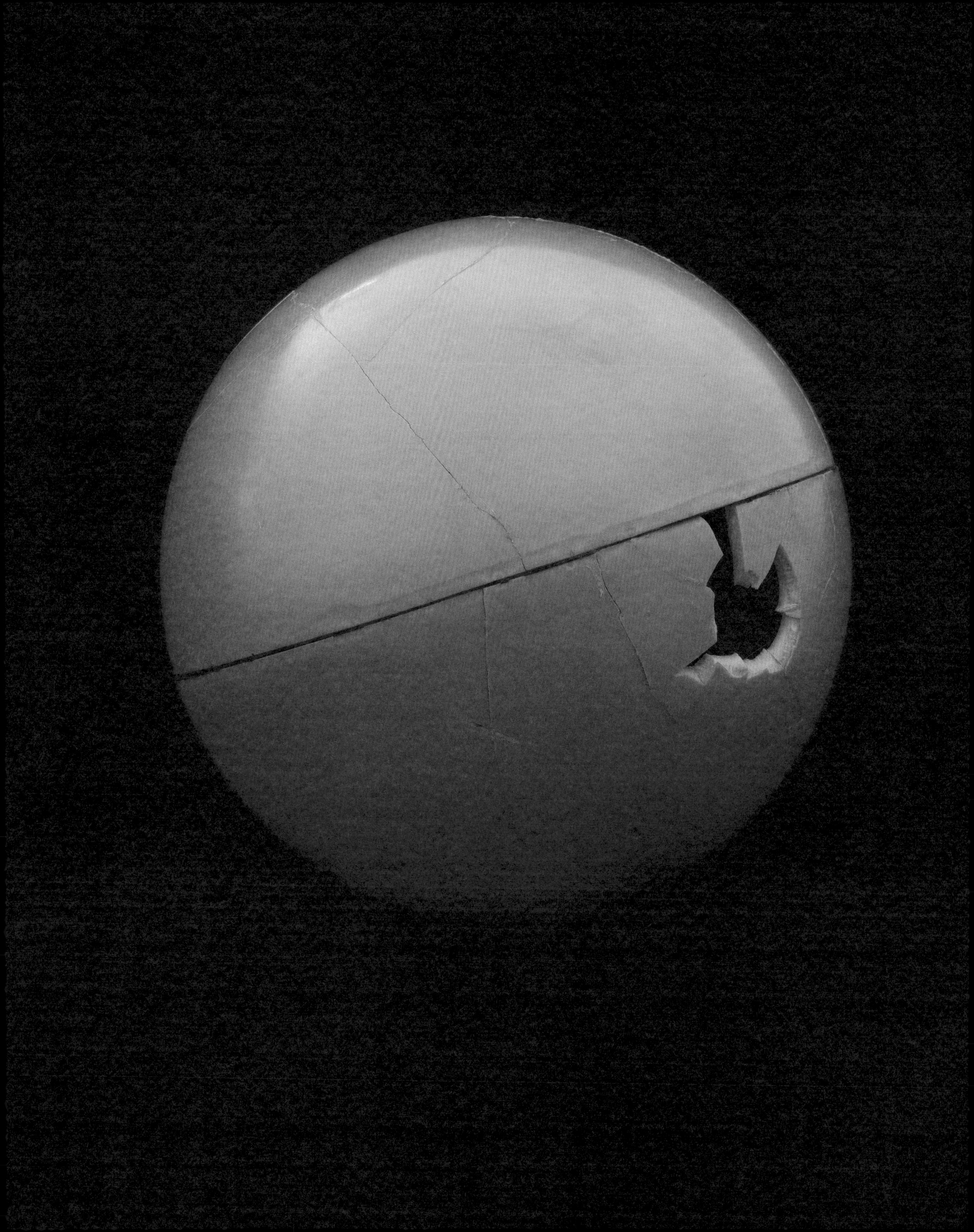

Skull C.B. 1

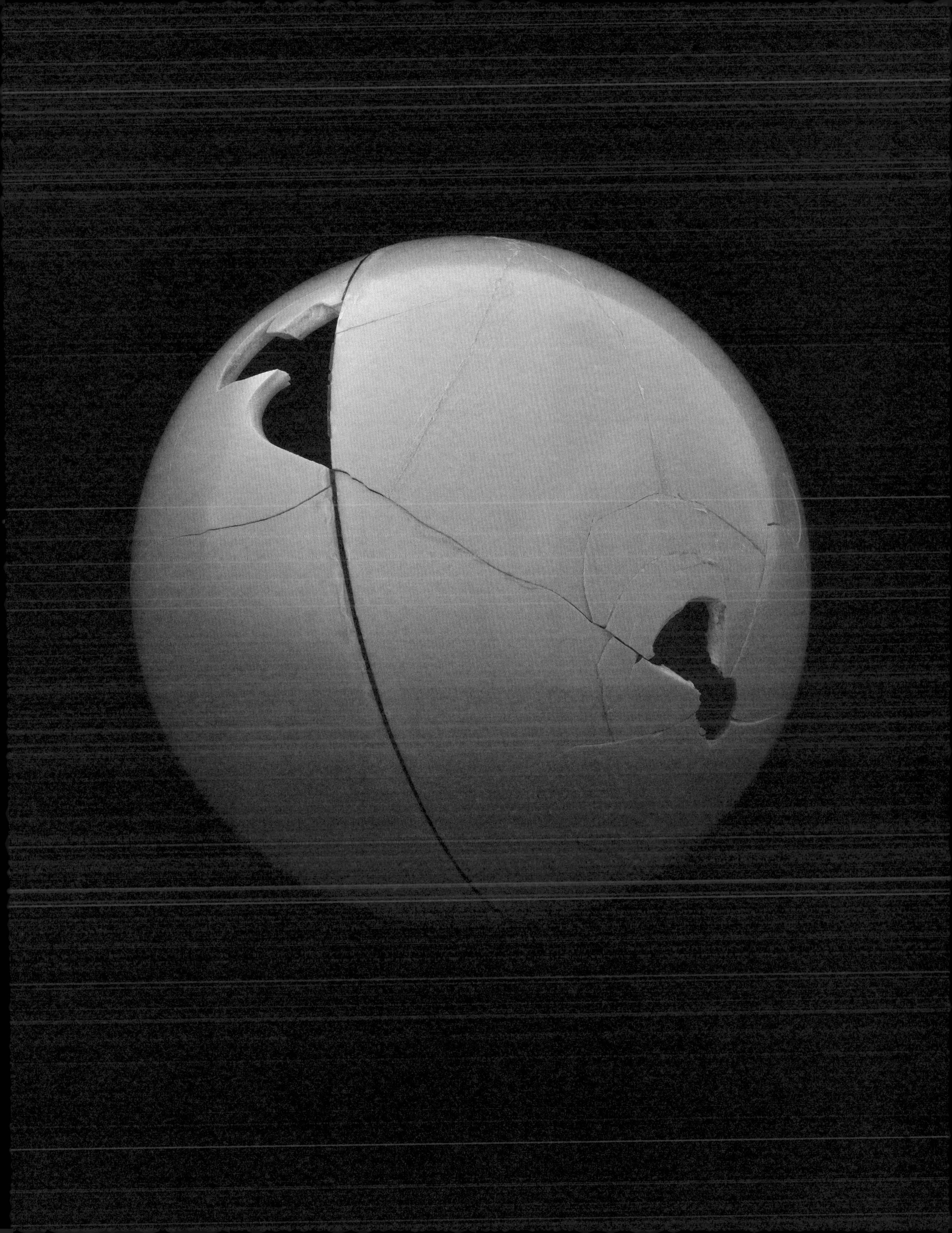

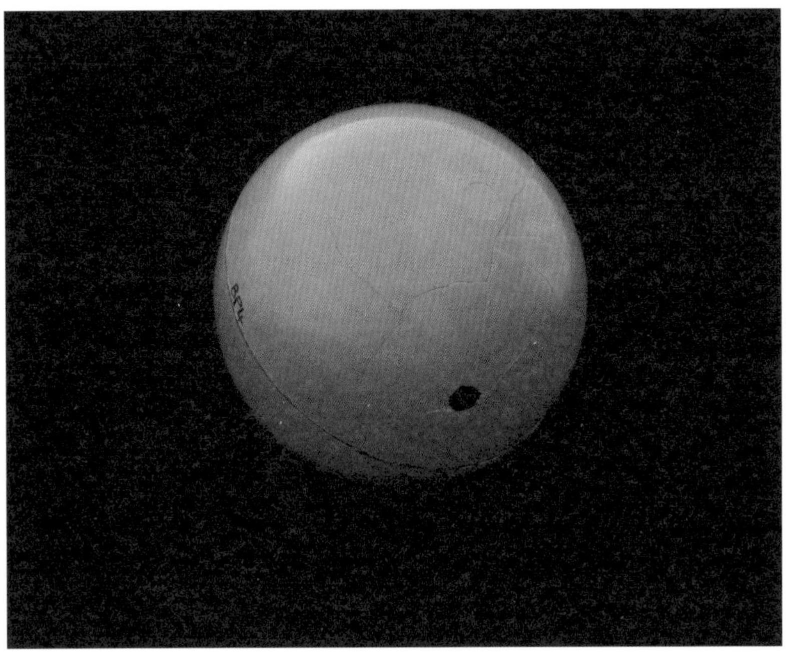

Skull B.P. 4

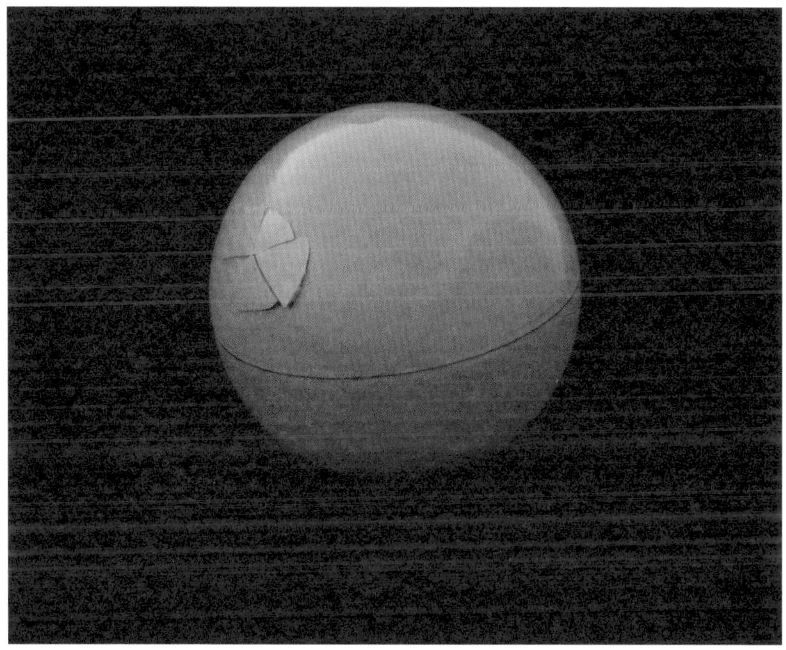

Skull C.B. 2

BONHEUR

2019

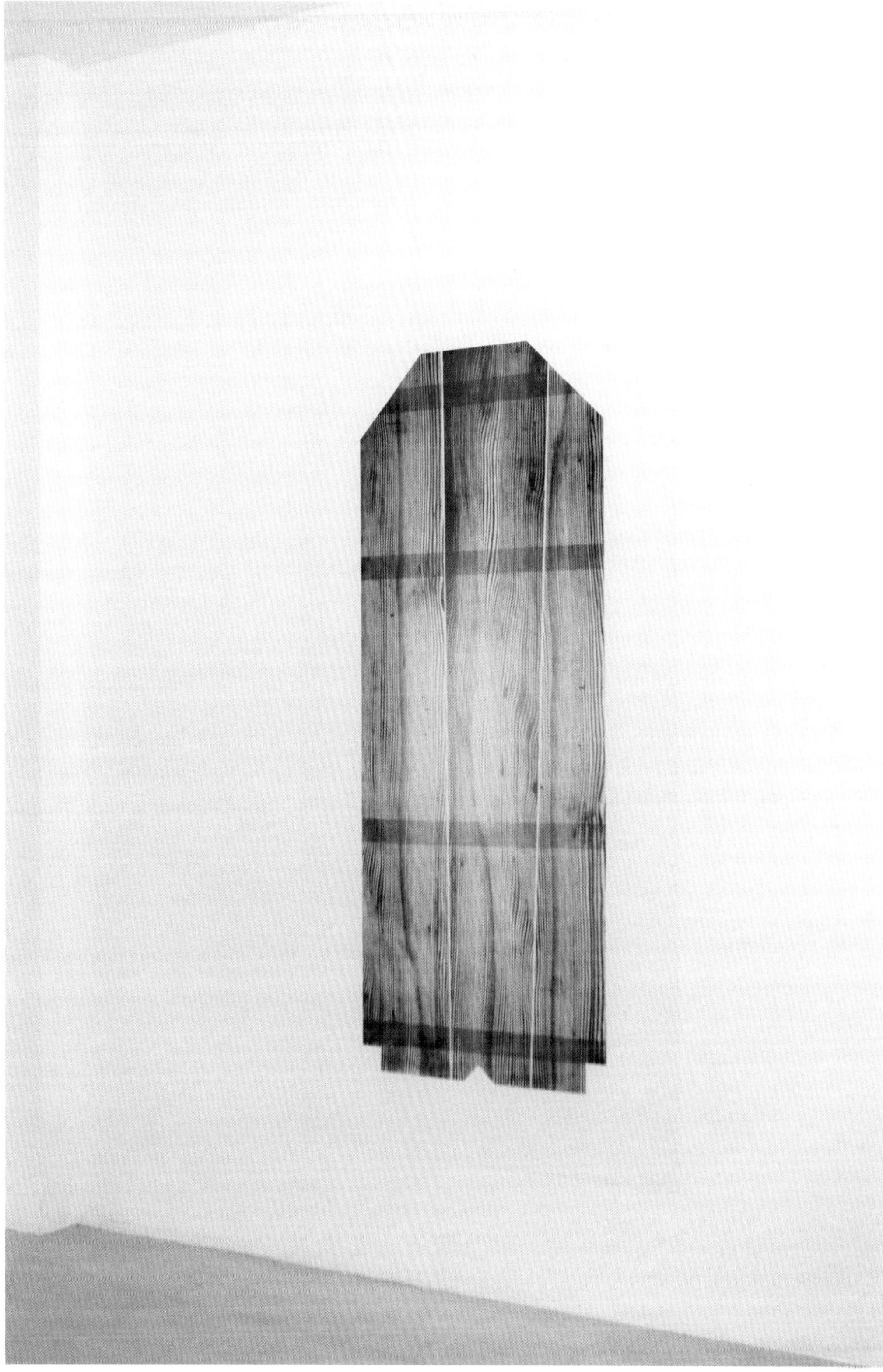

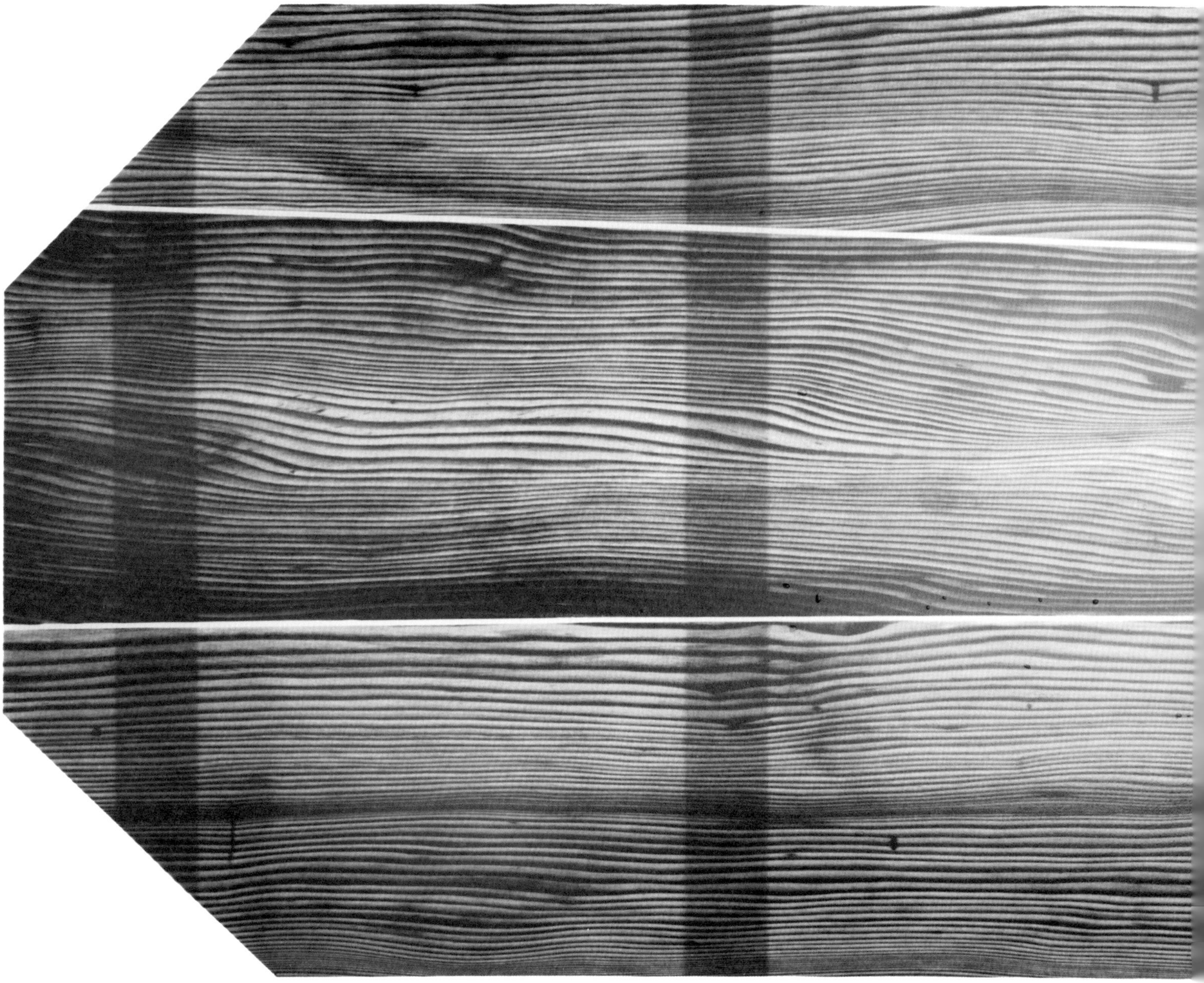

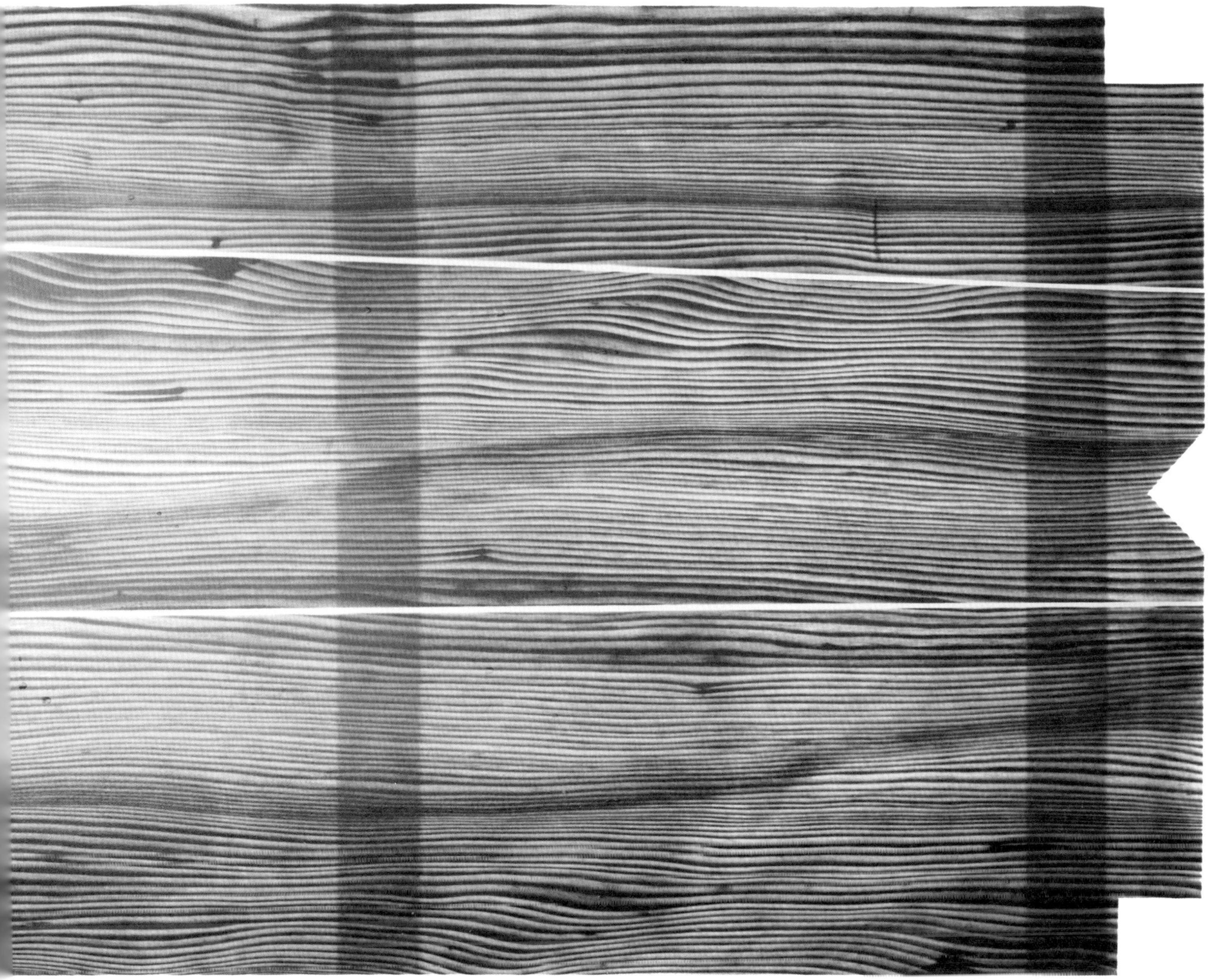

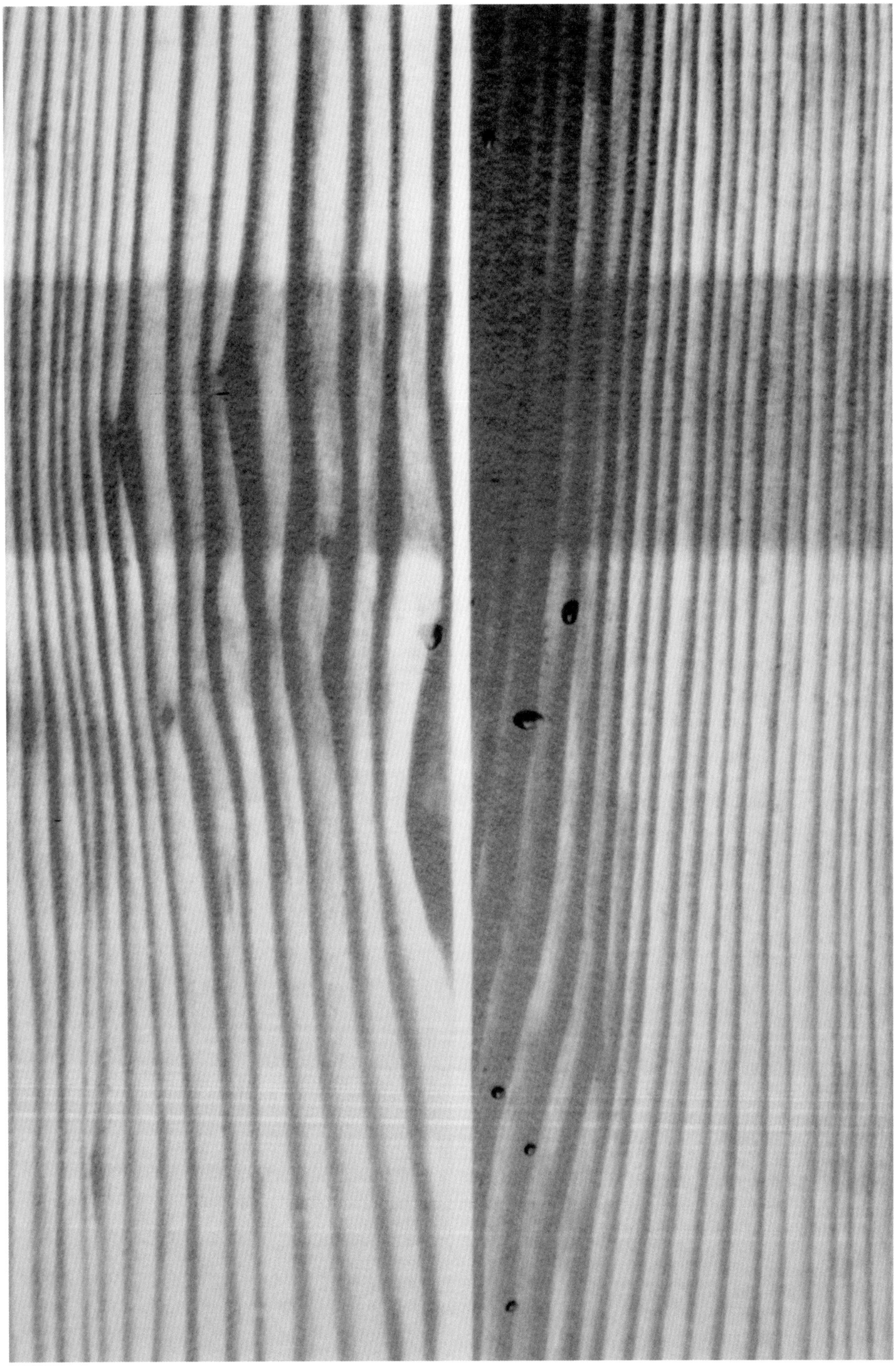

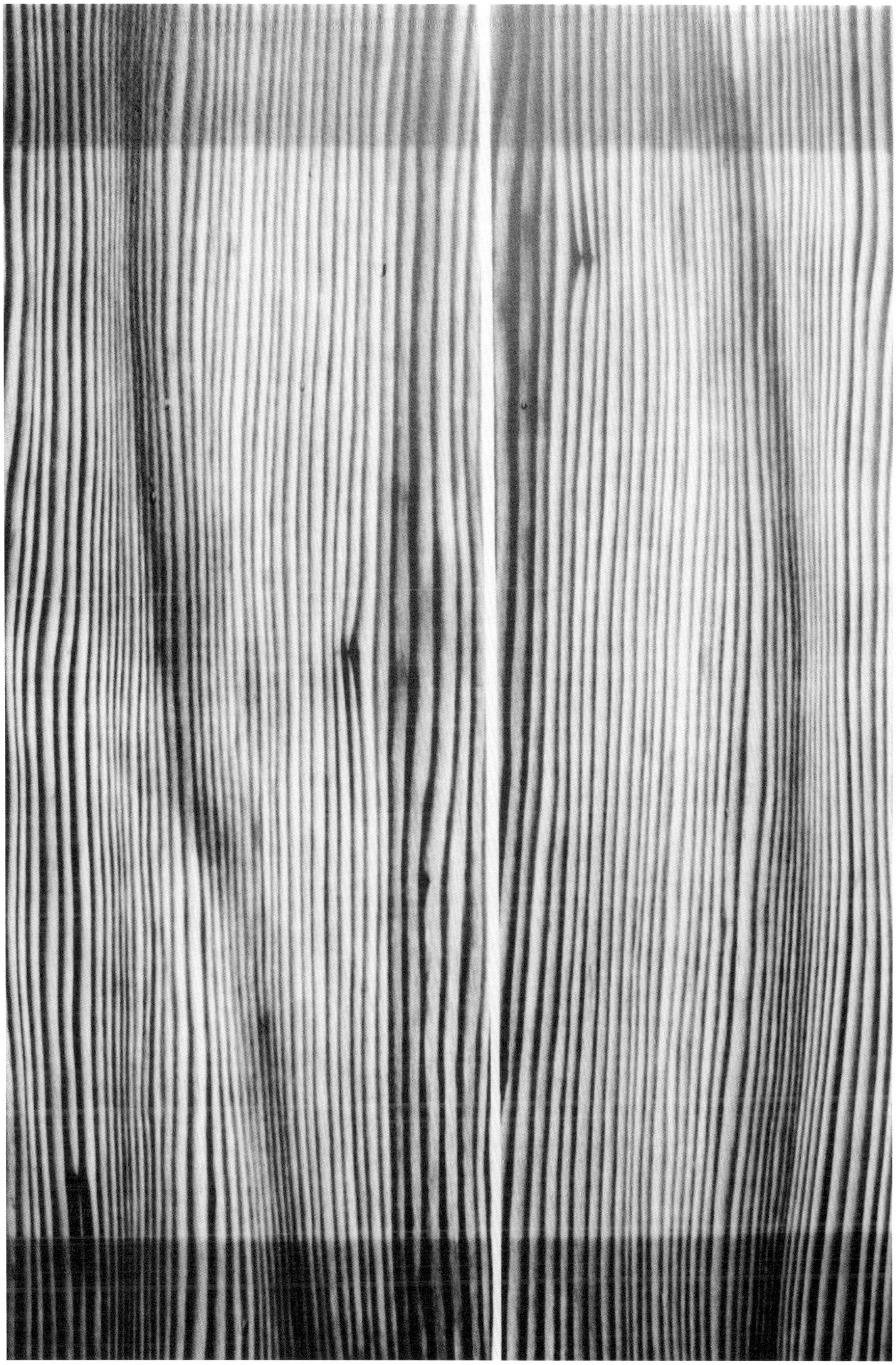

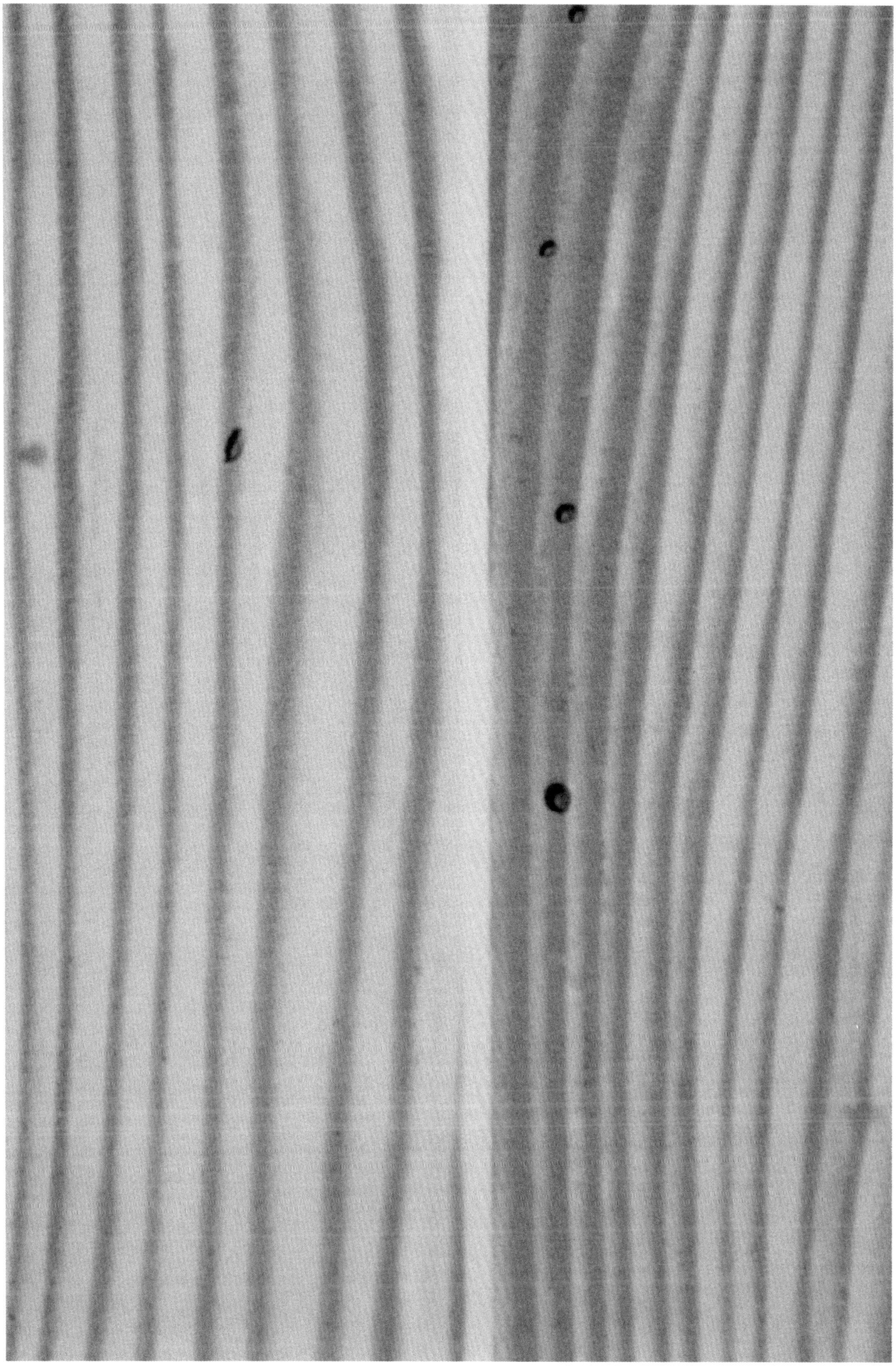

SHADOW IS A HOLE

2021-2023

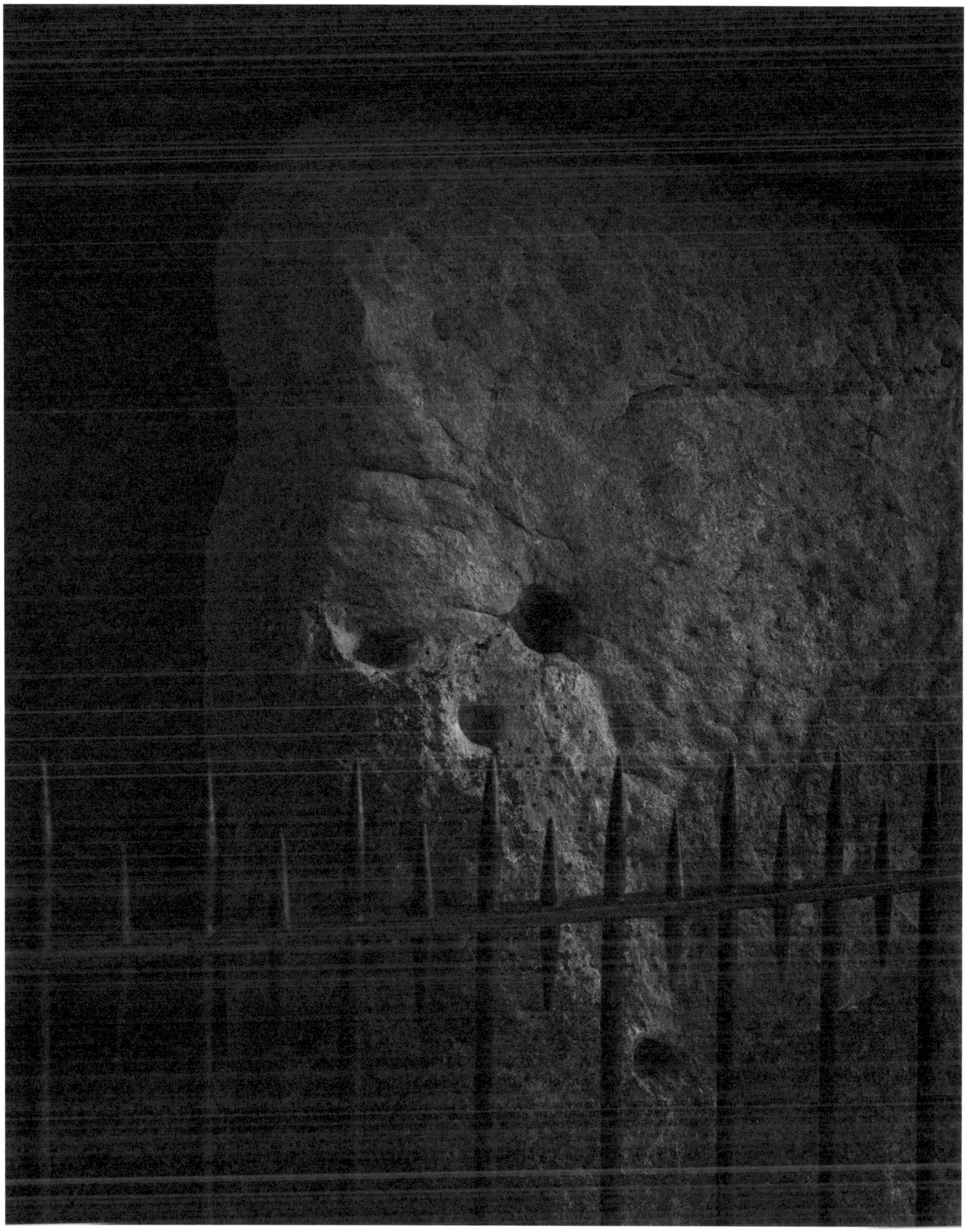

Fence

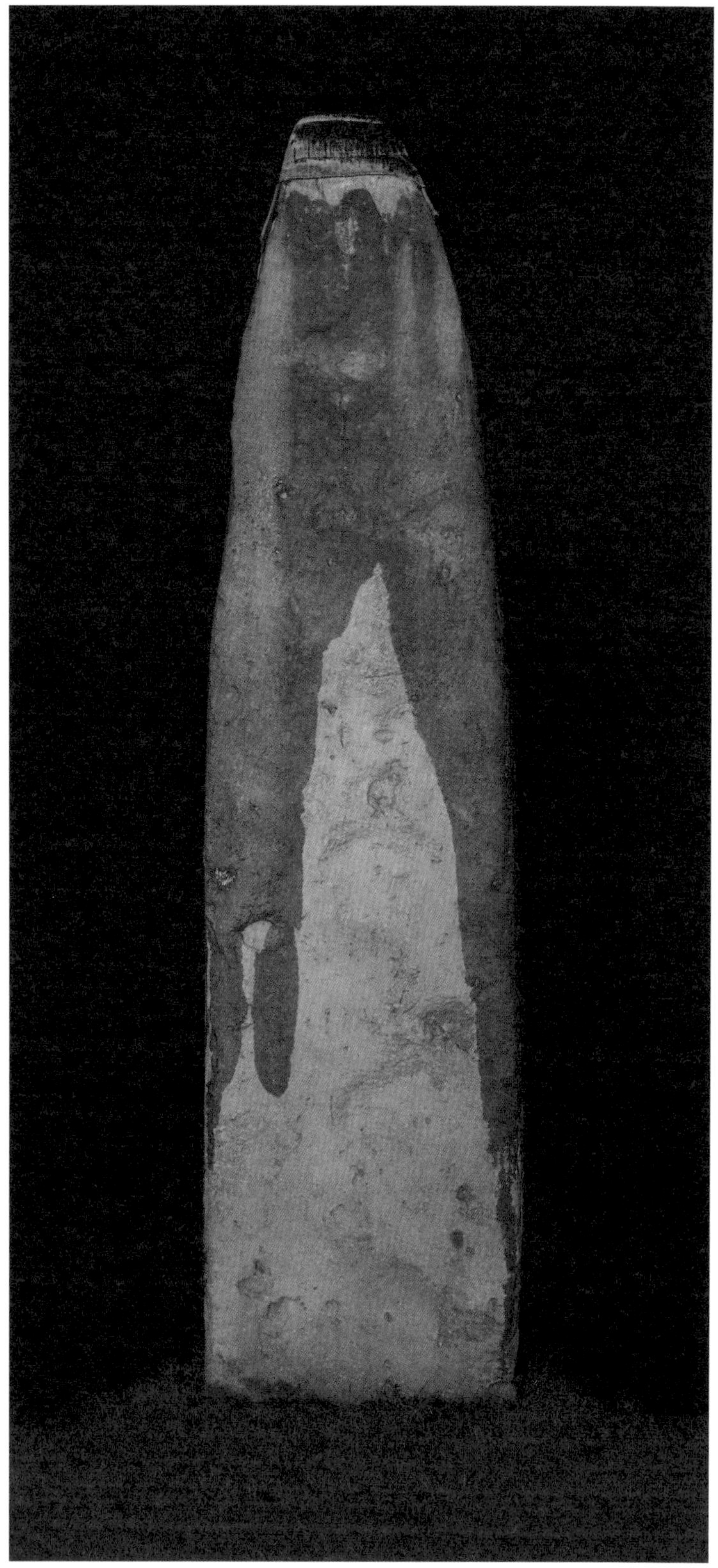

Monolith

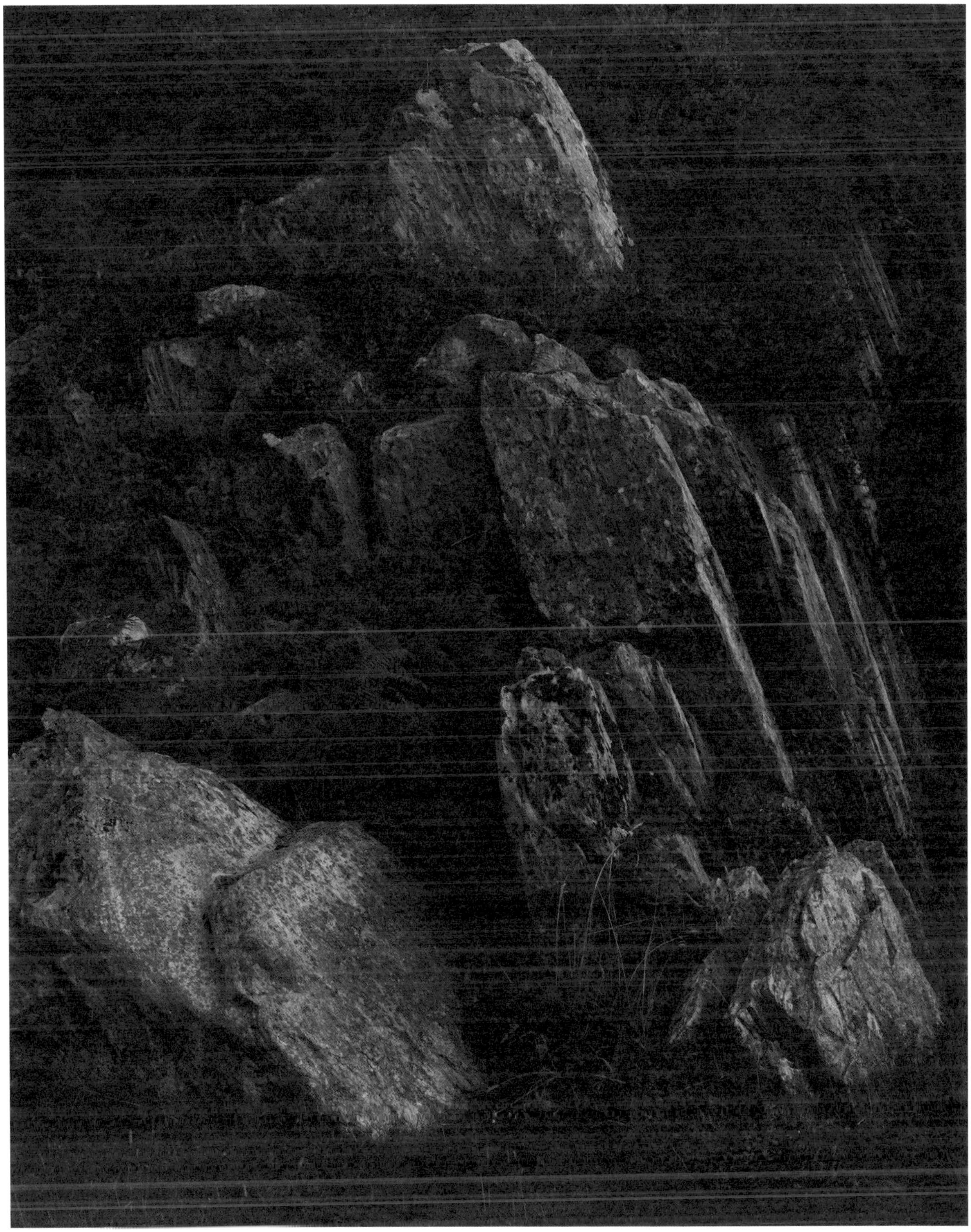

Rock formation

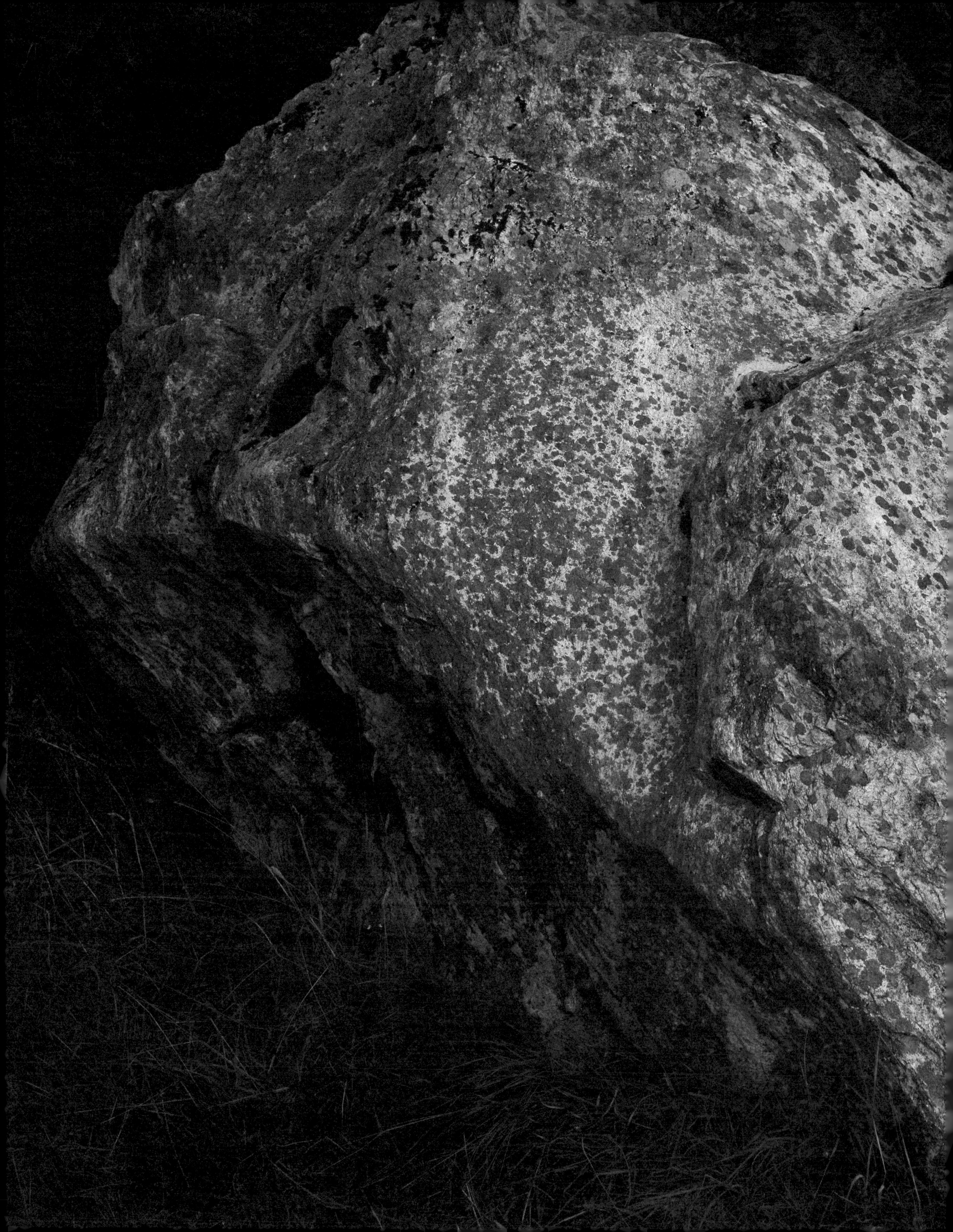

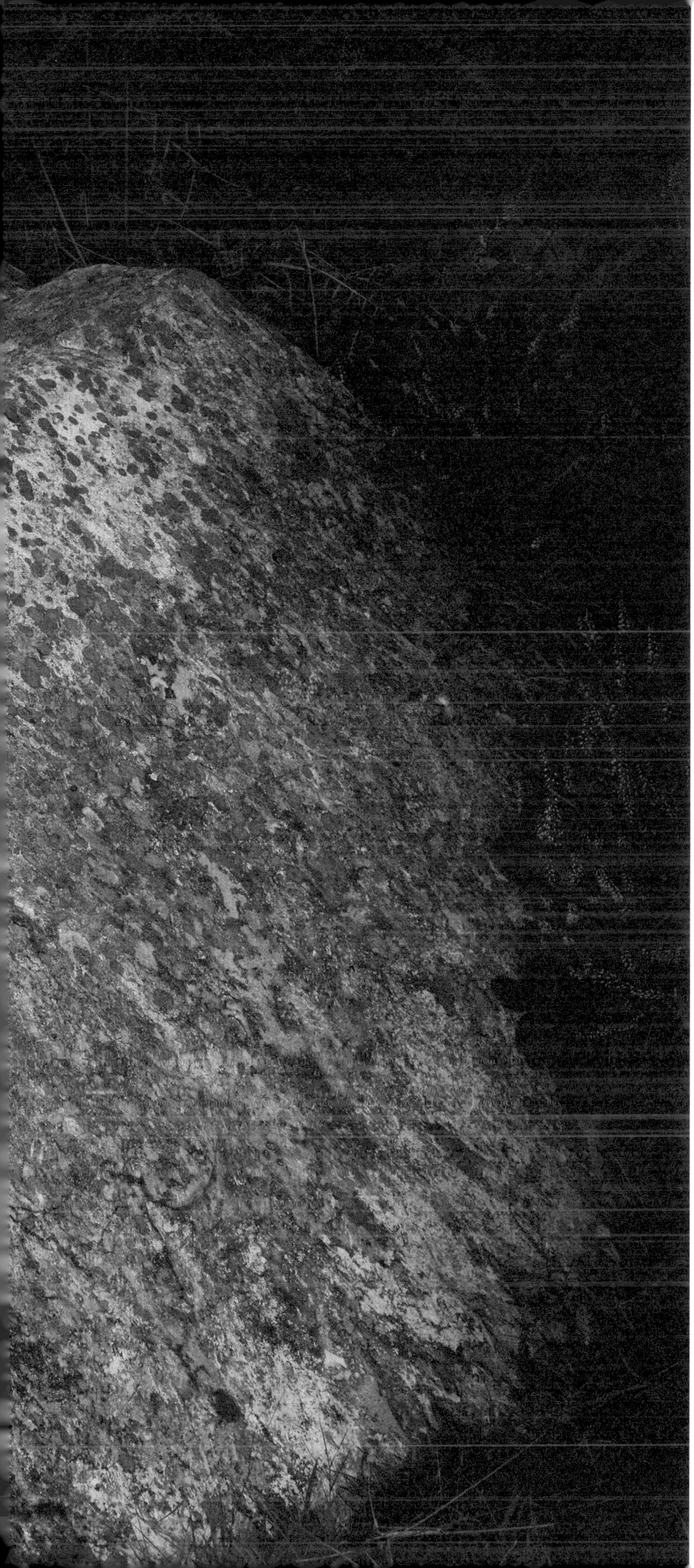

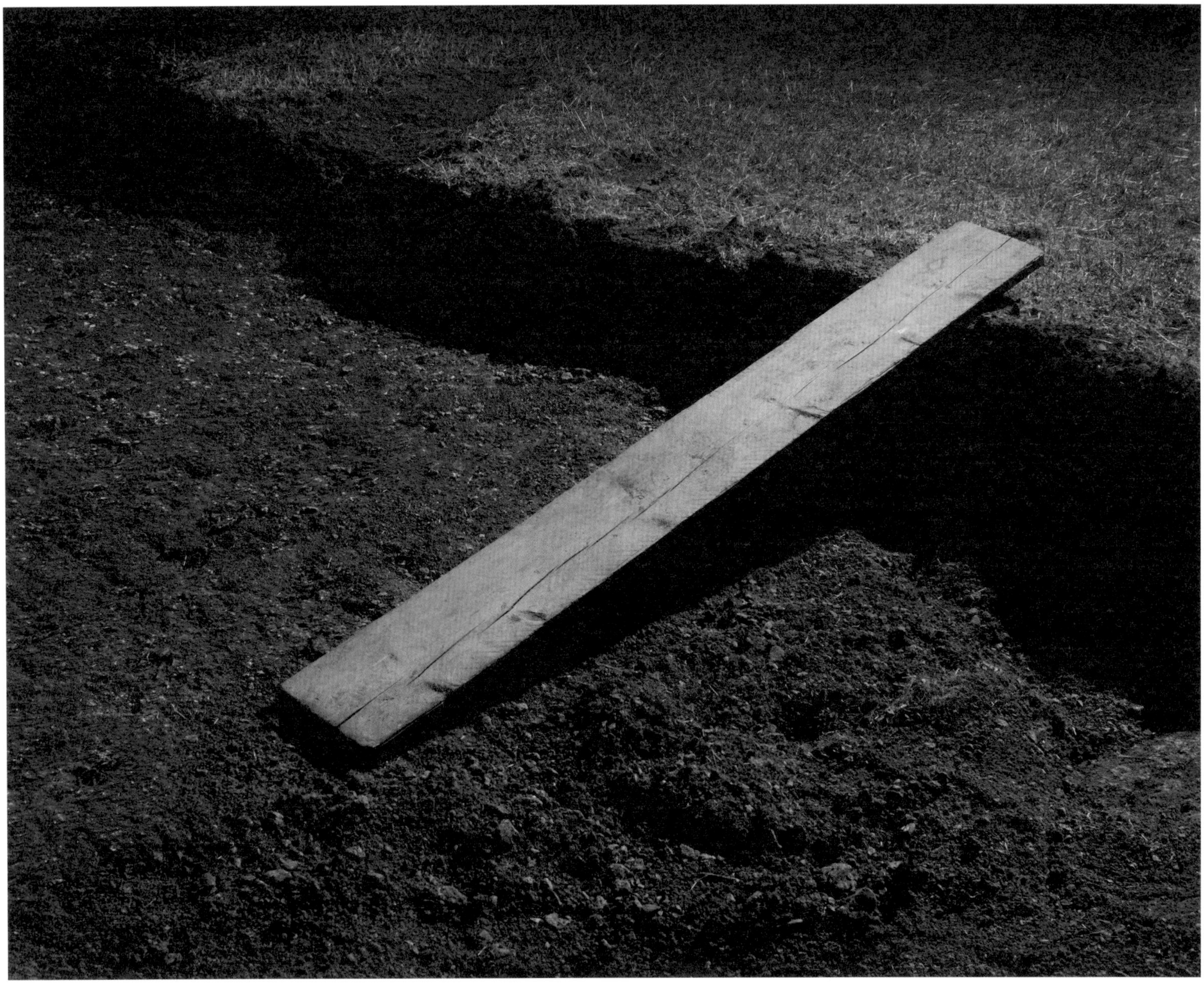

Shelf

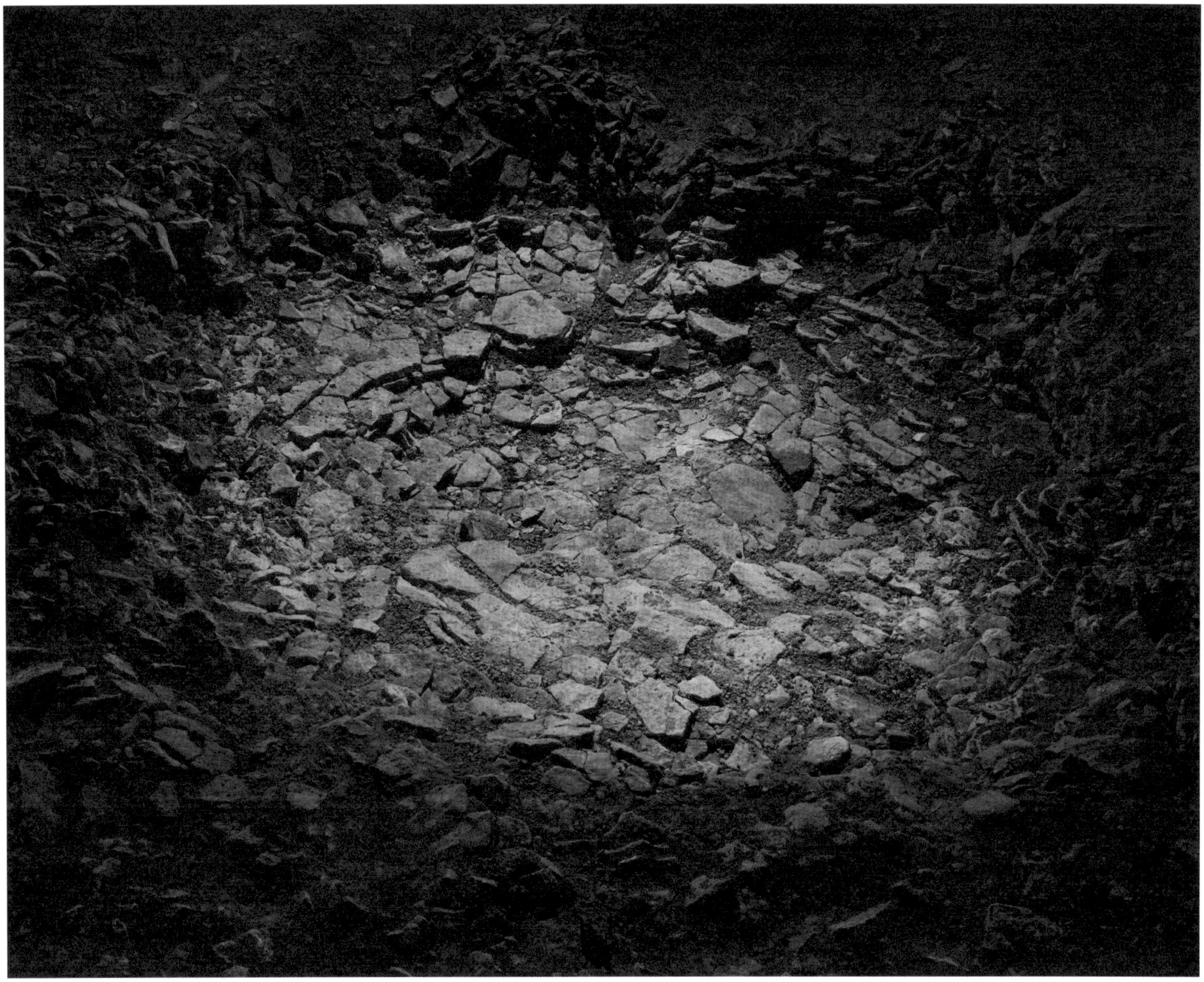

Quarry

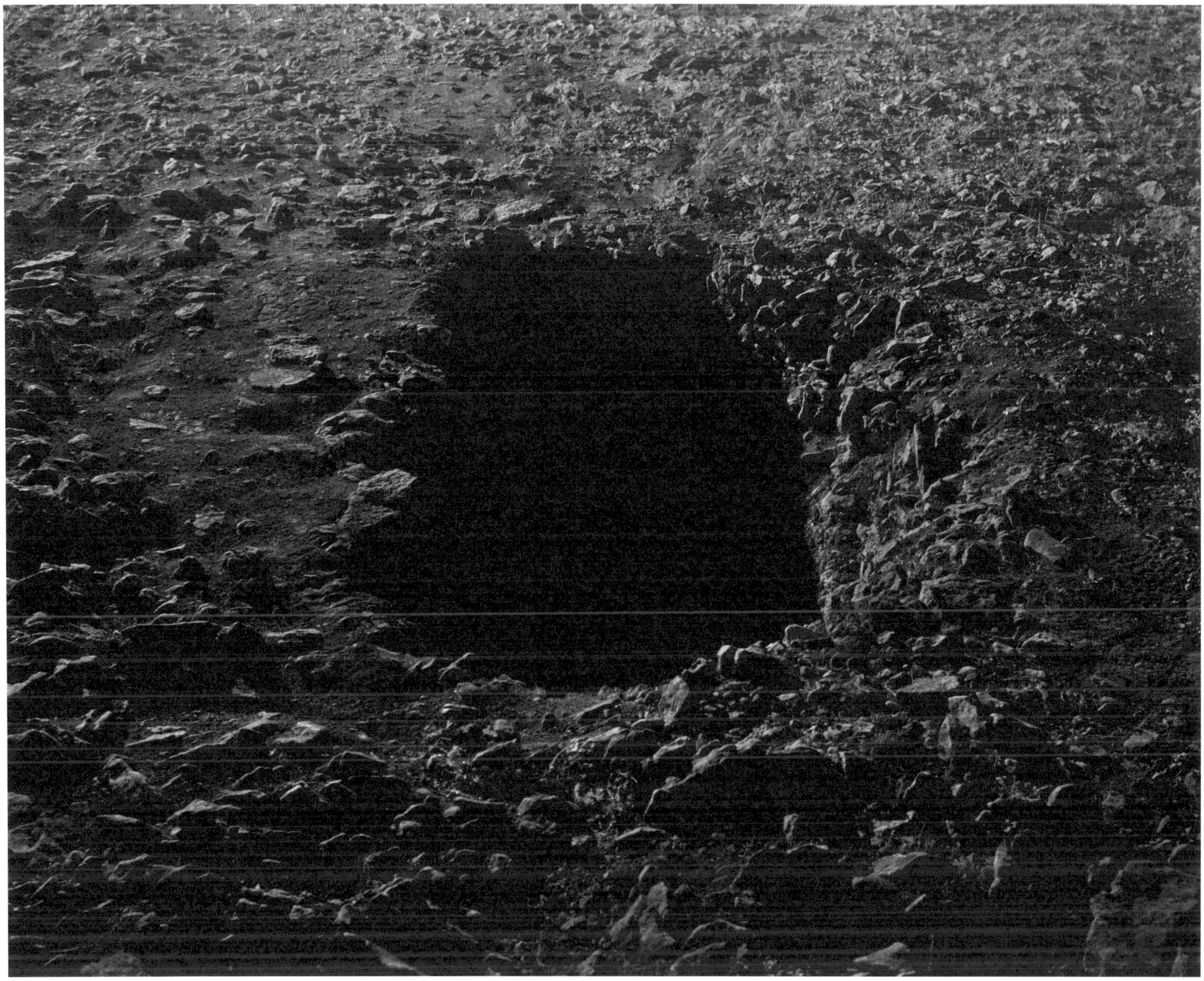

Ash hole

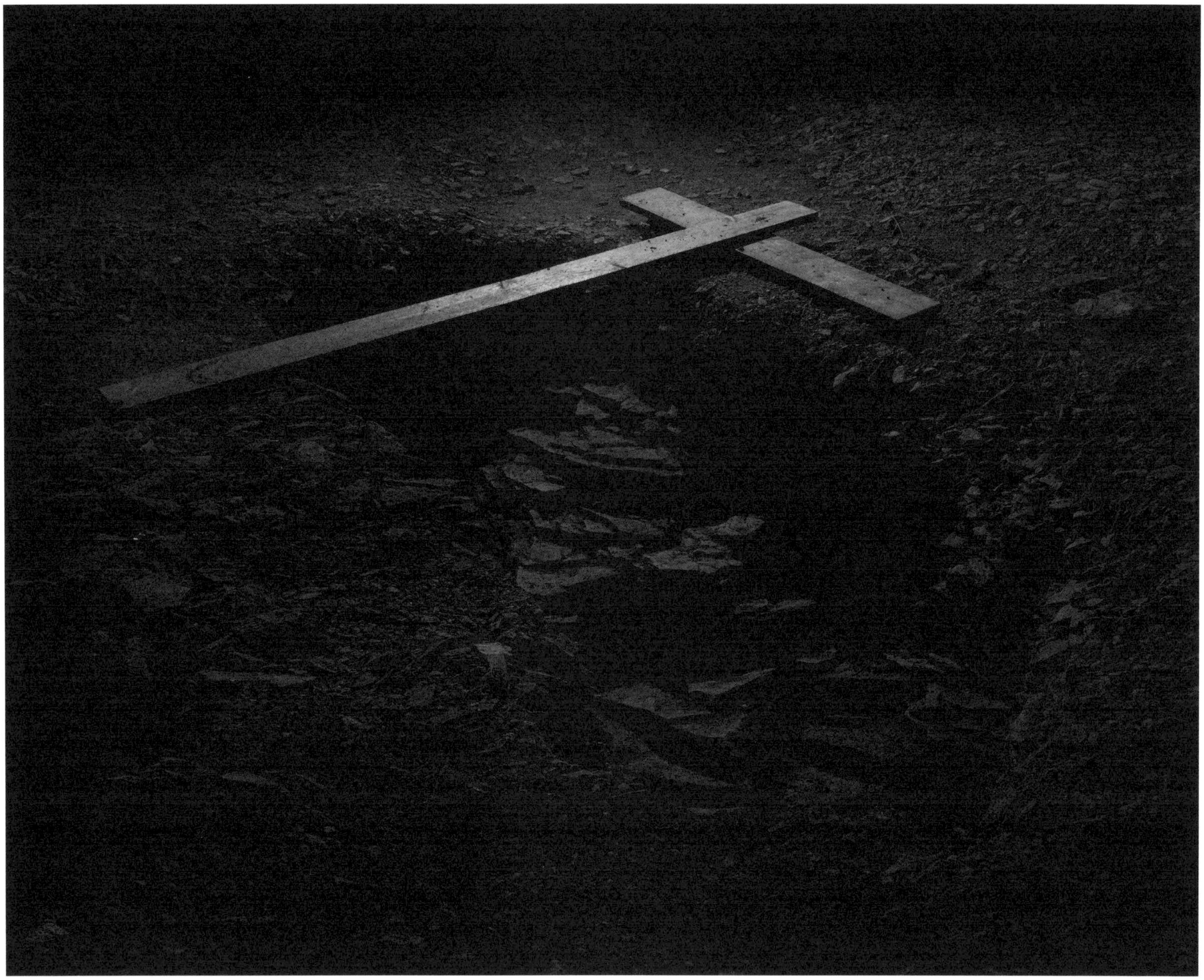

Crossing

Path

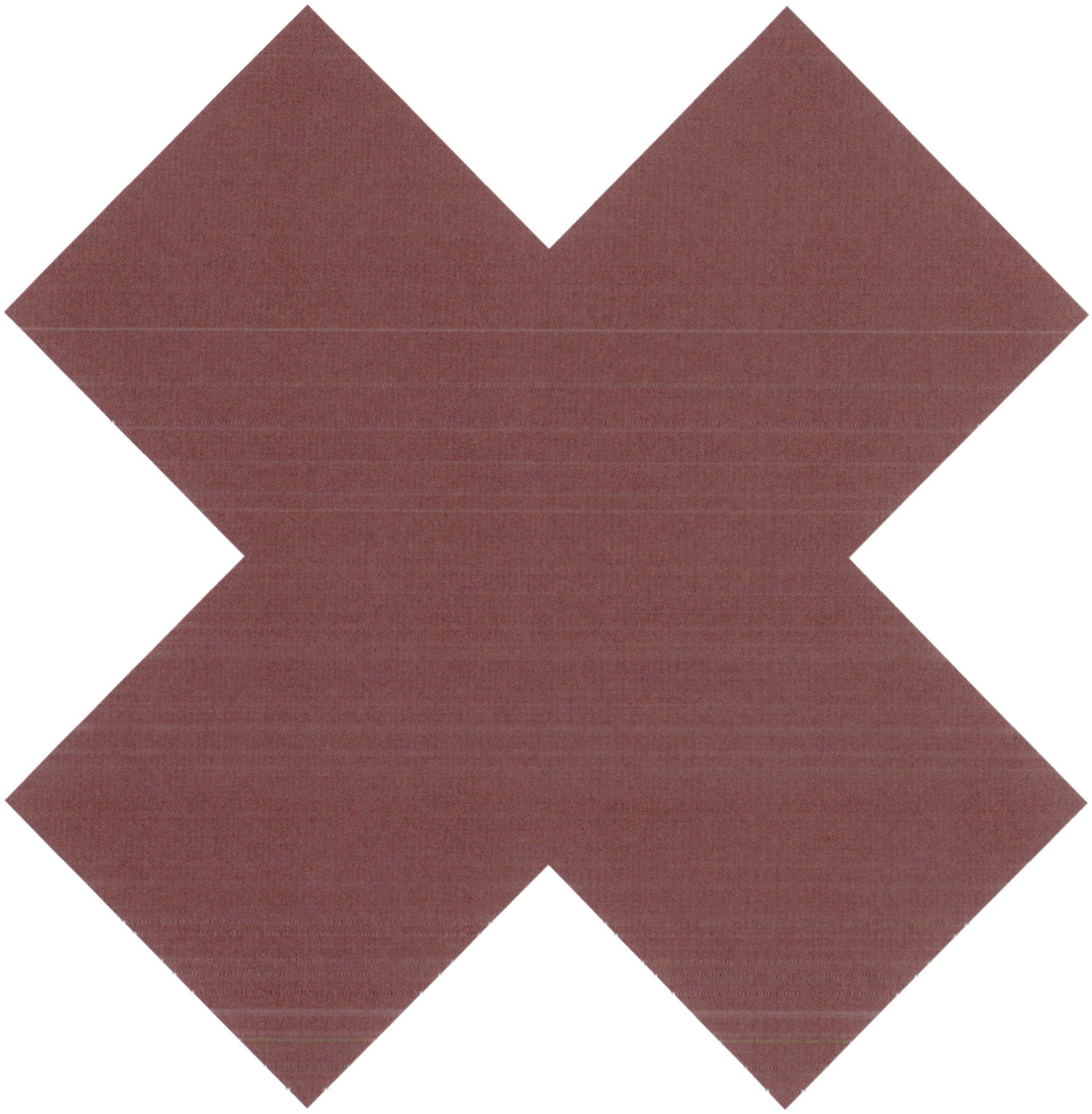

EXPO

TER POSTERIE

2024

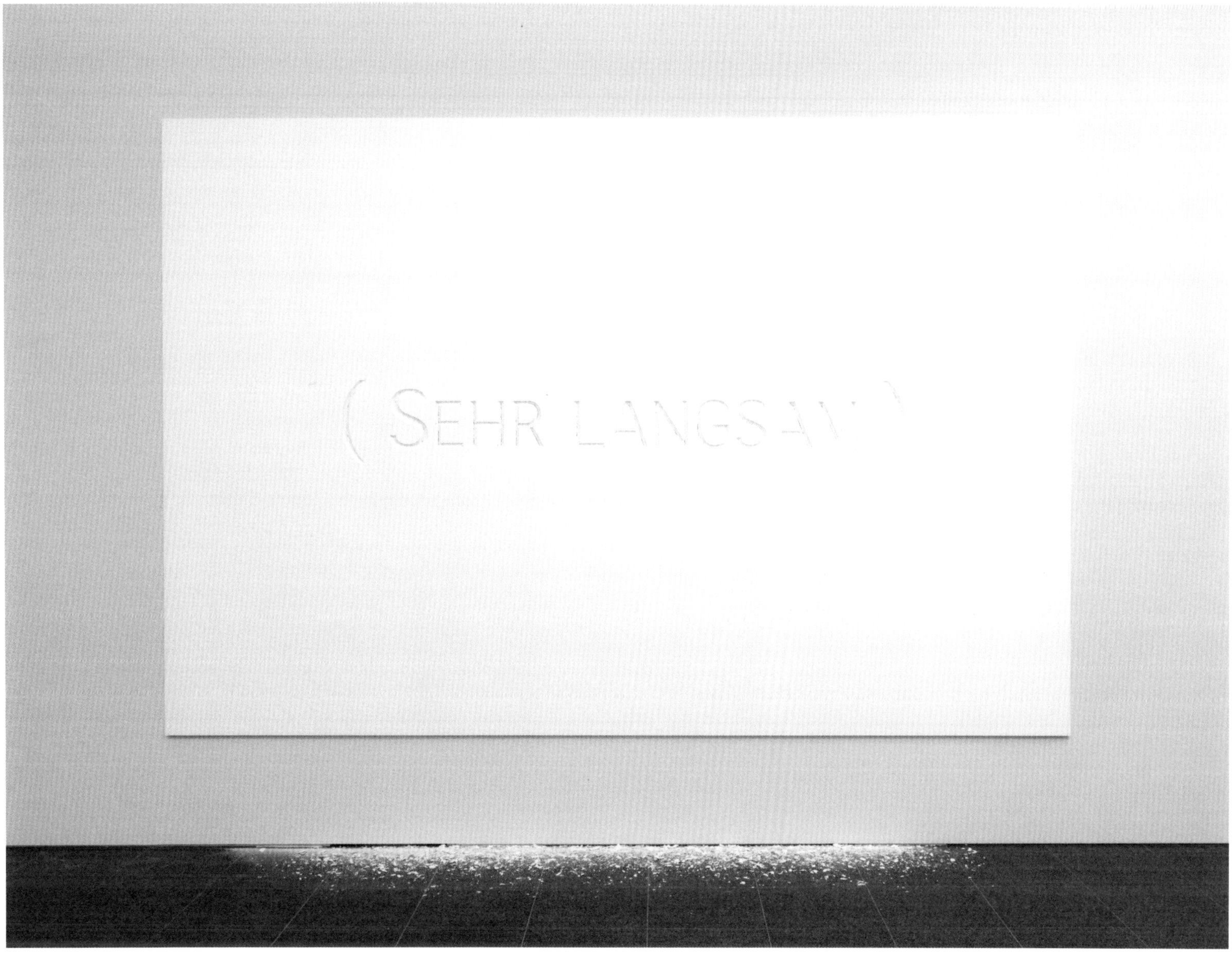
(SEHR LANGSAM

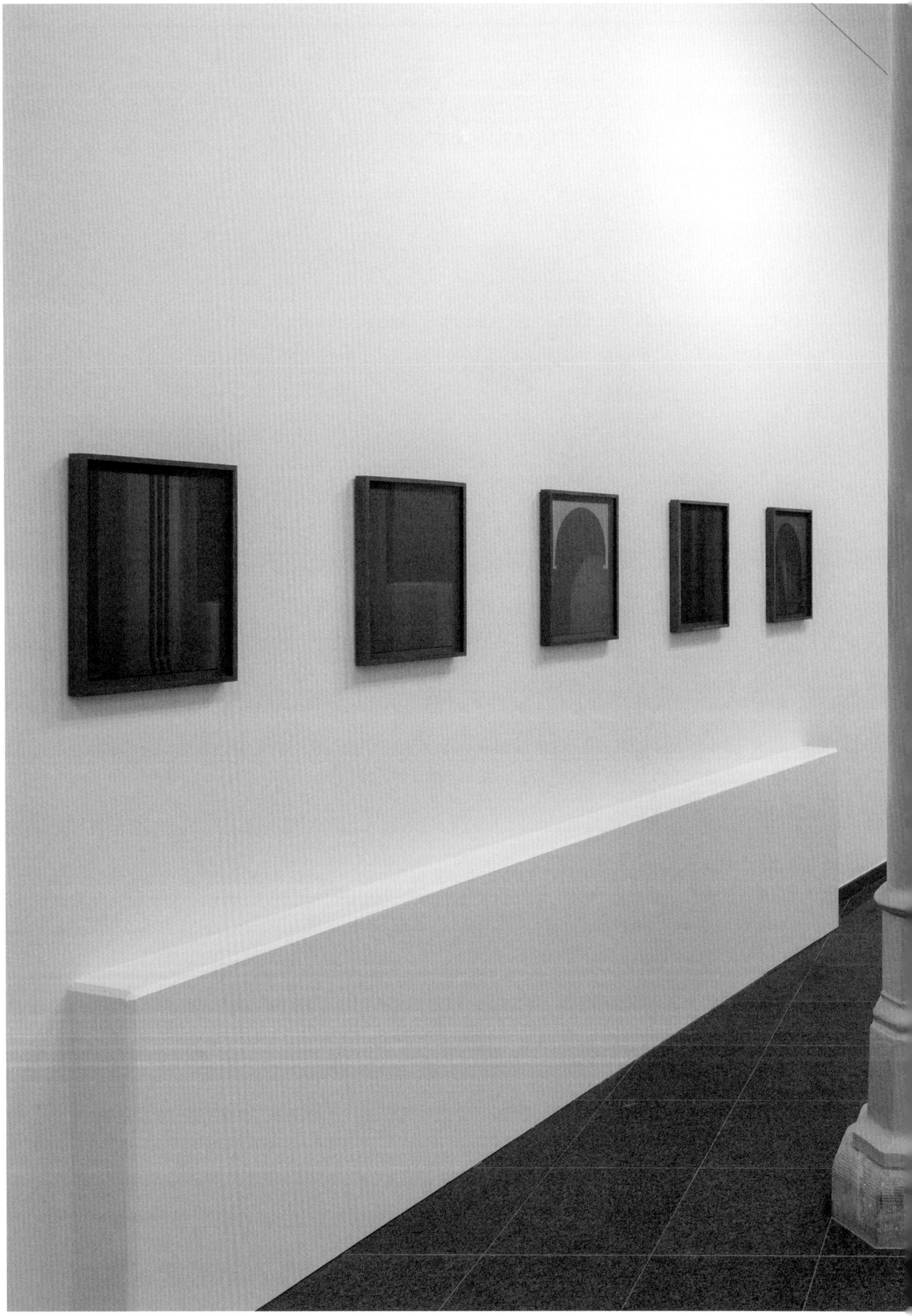

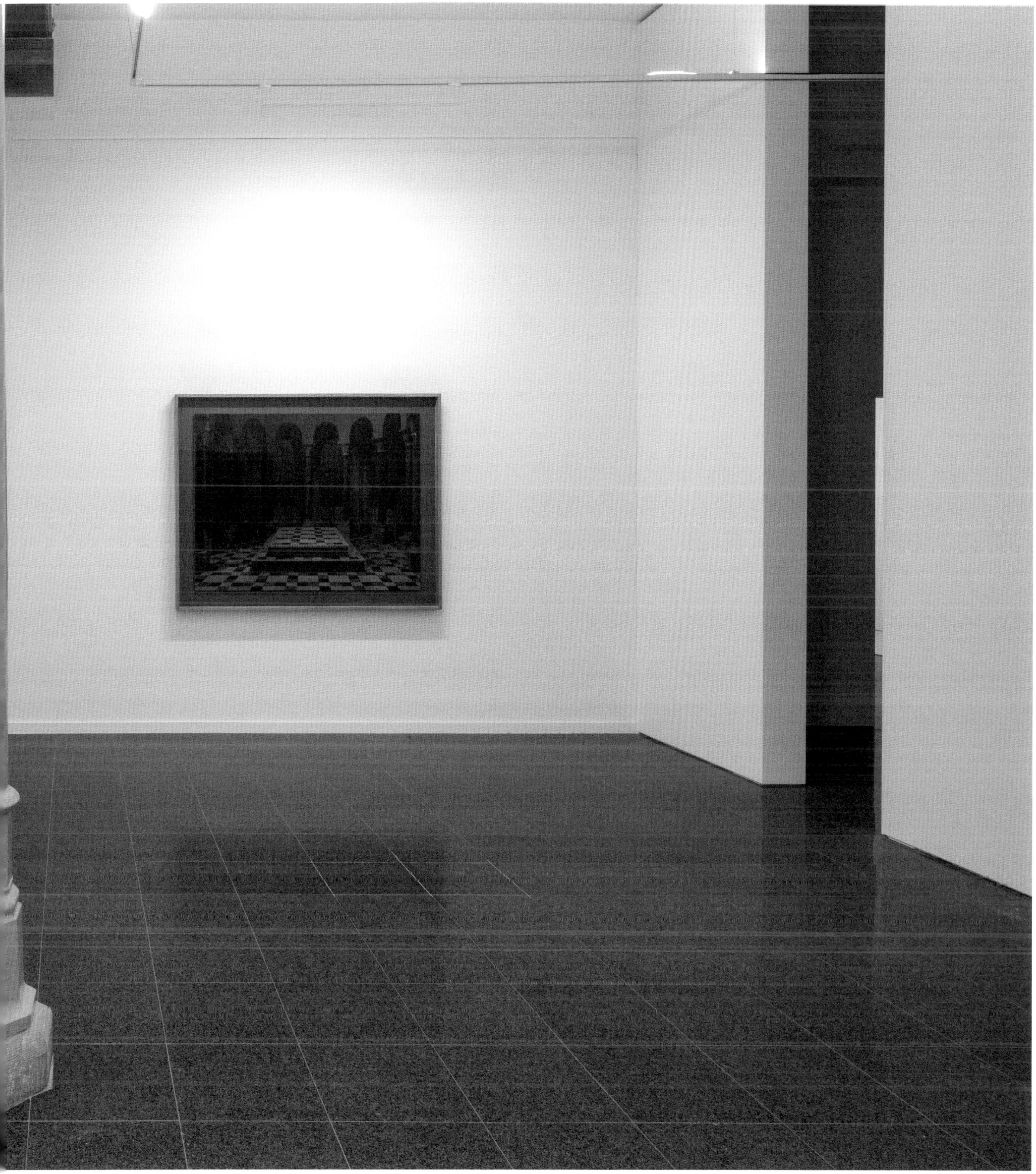

(SEHR LANGSAM)

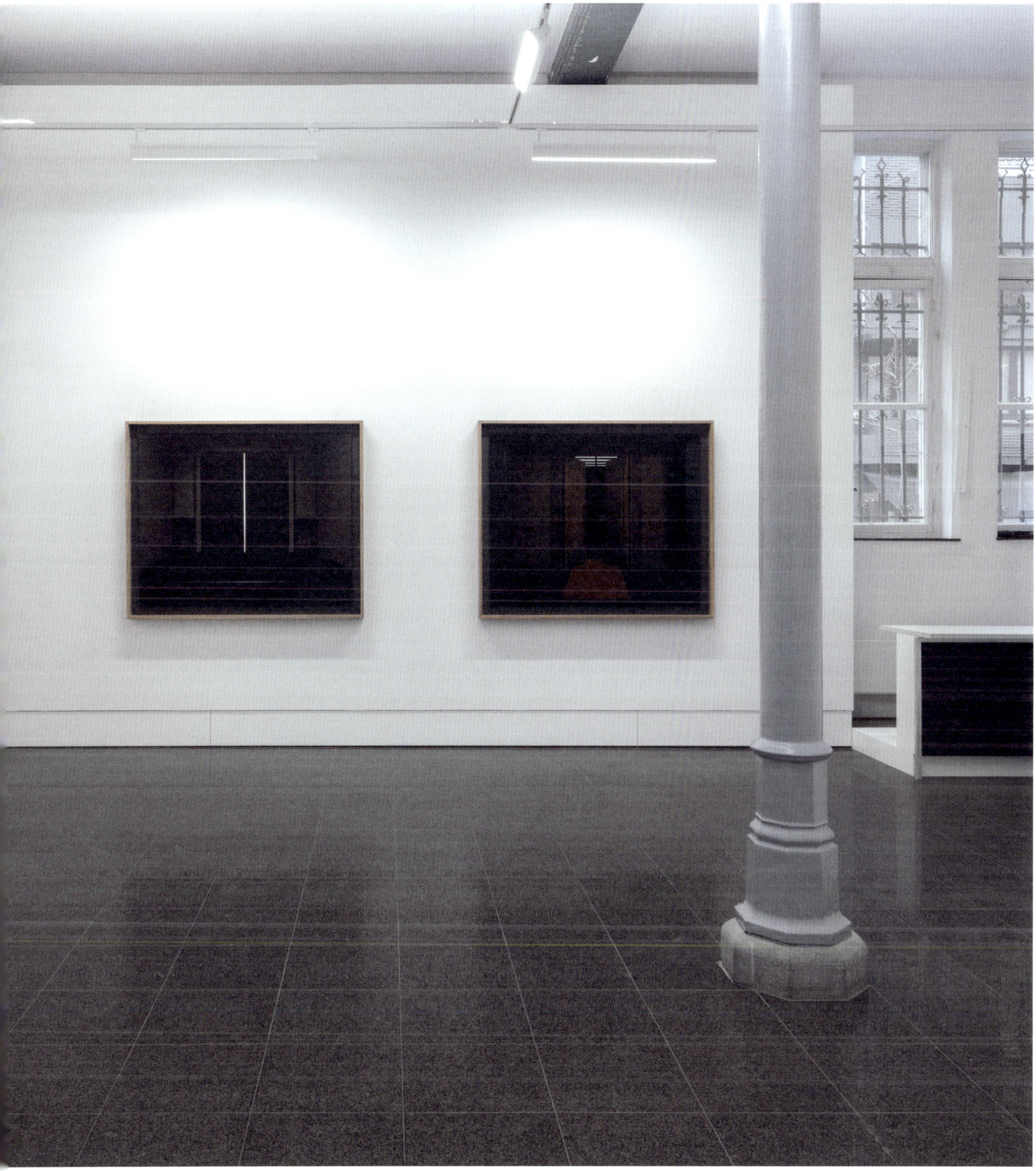

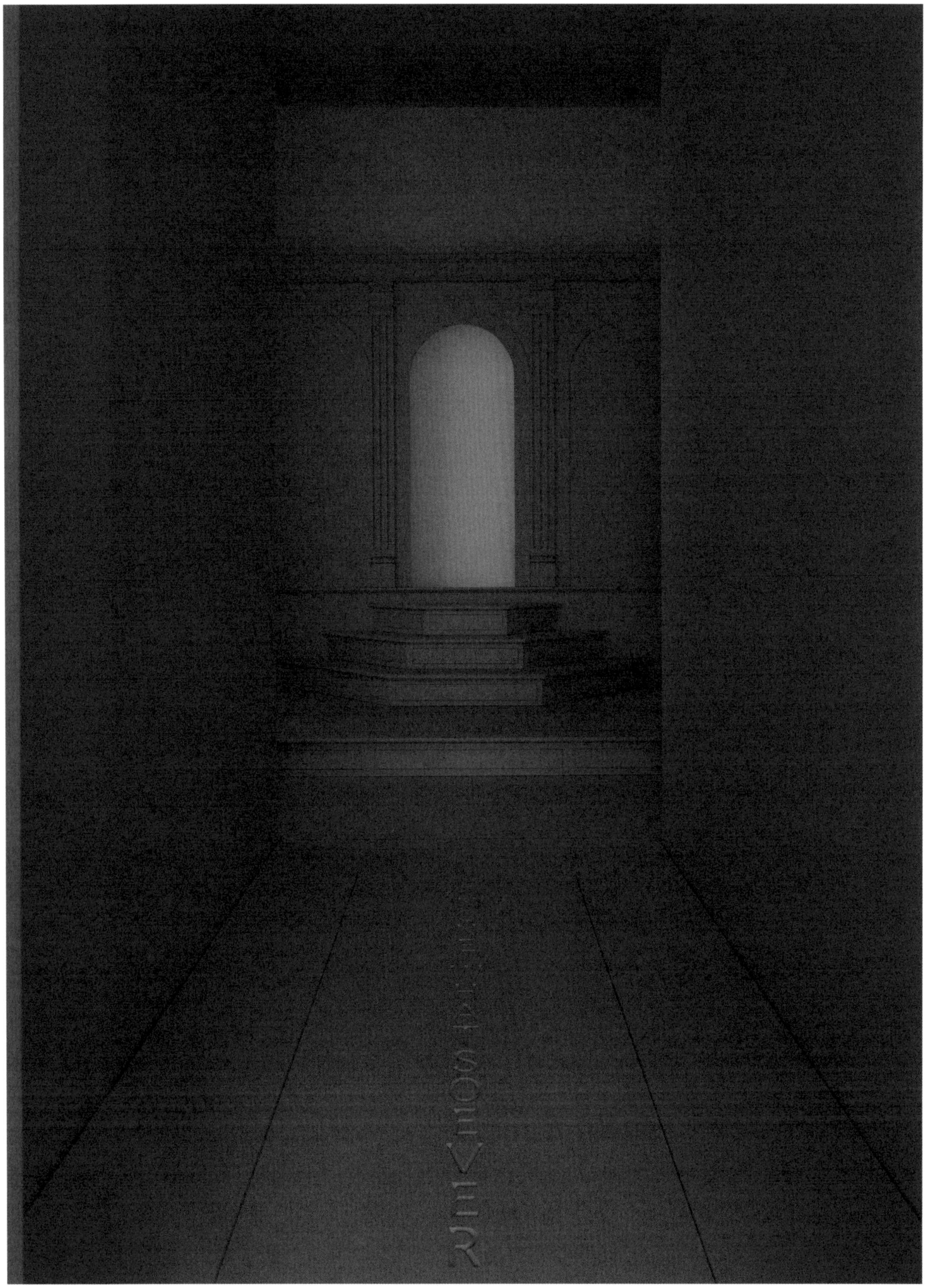

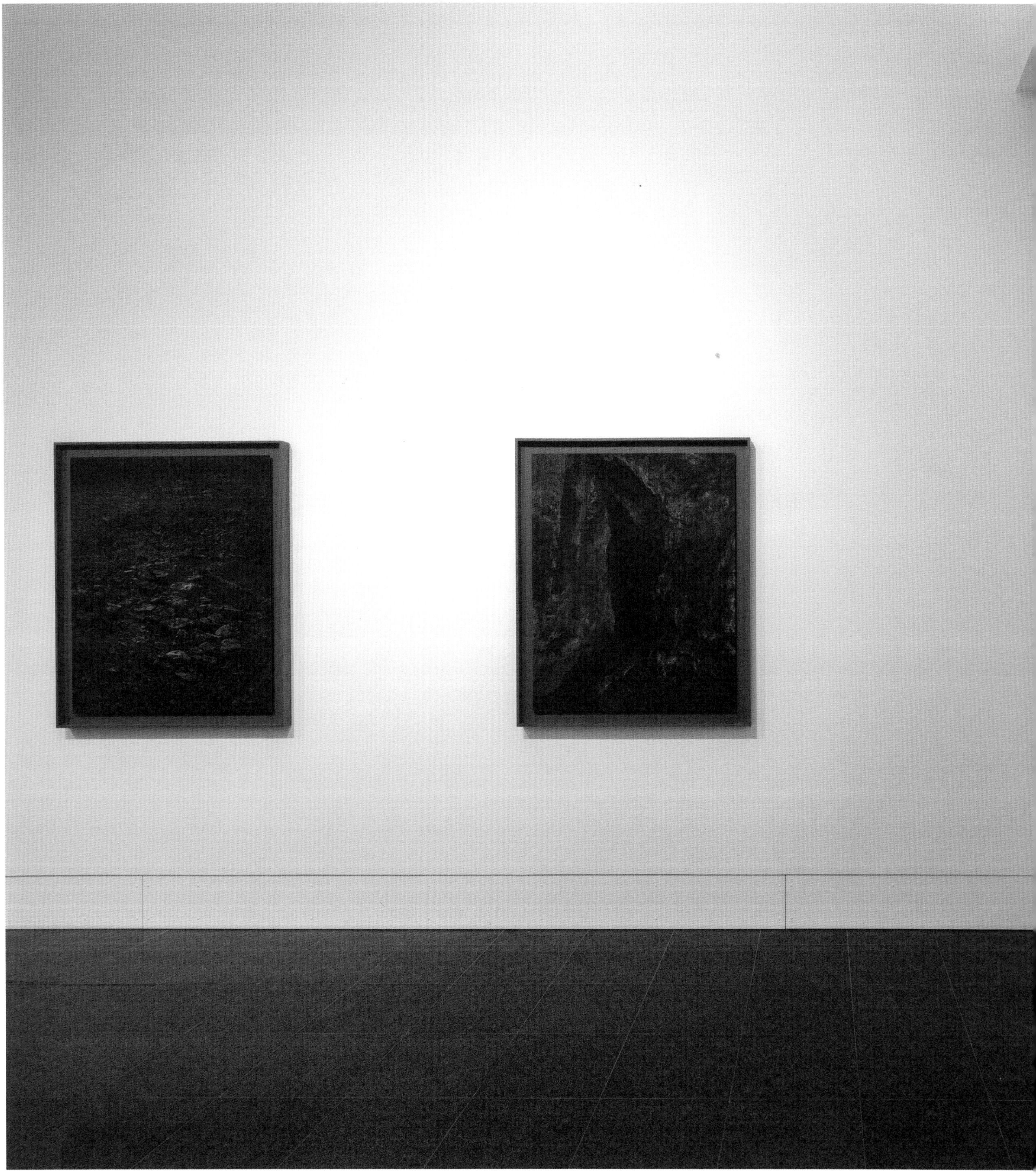

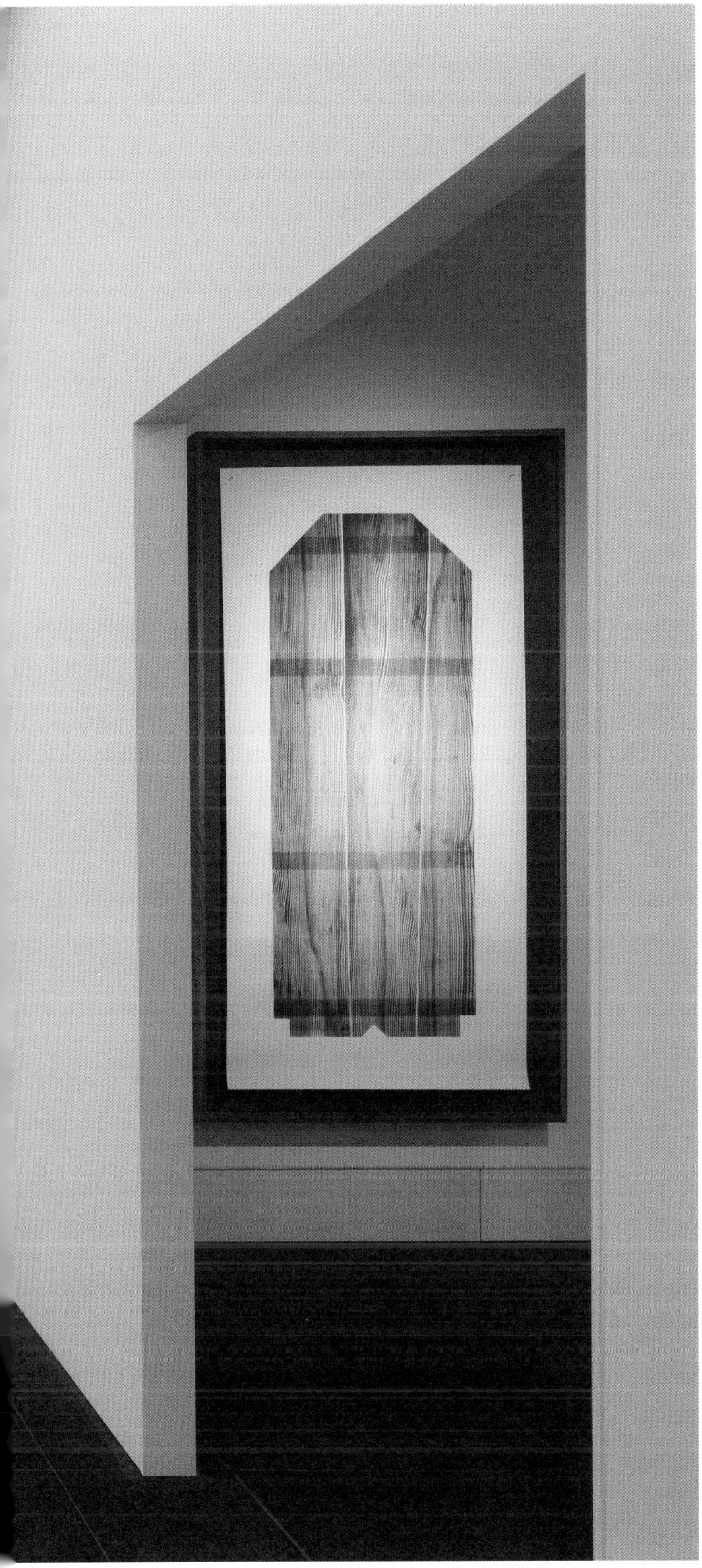

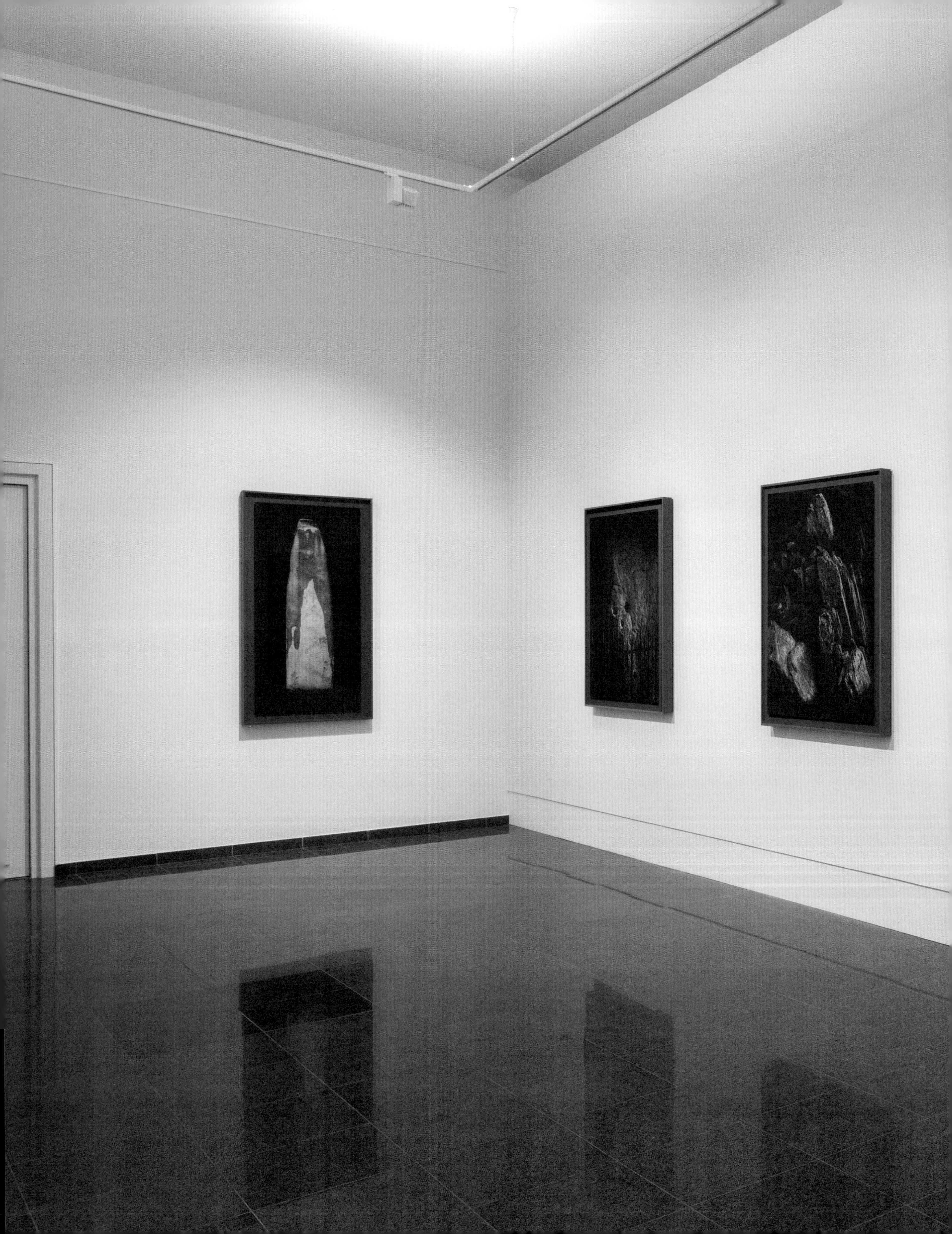

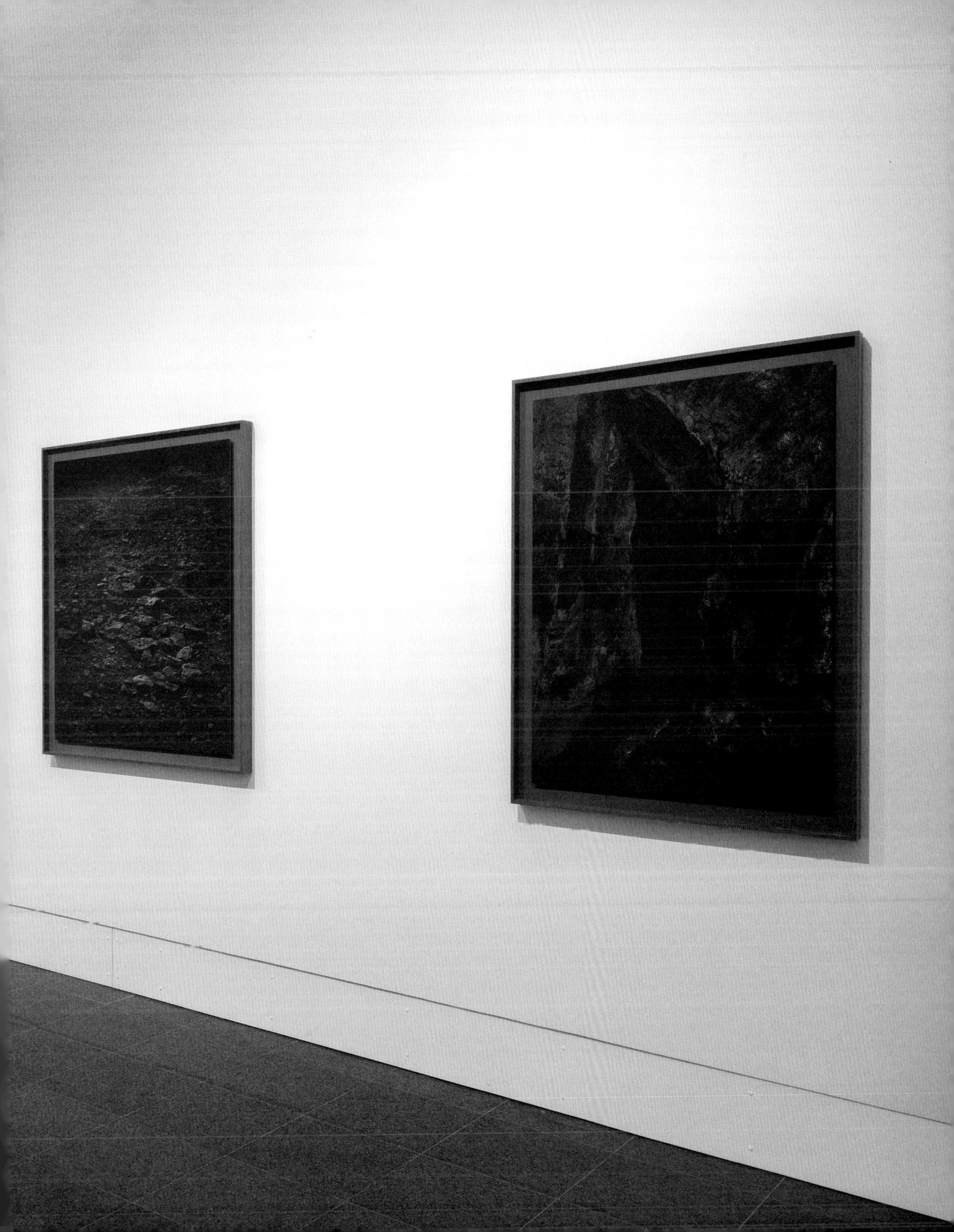

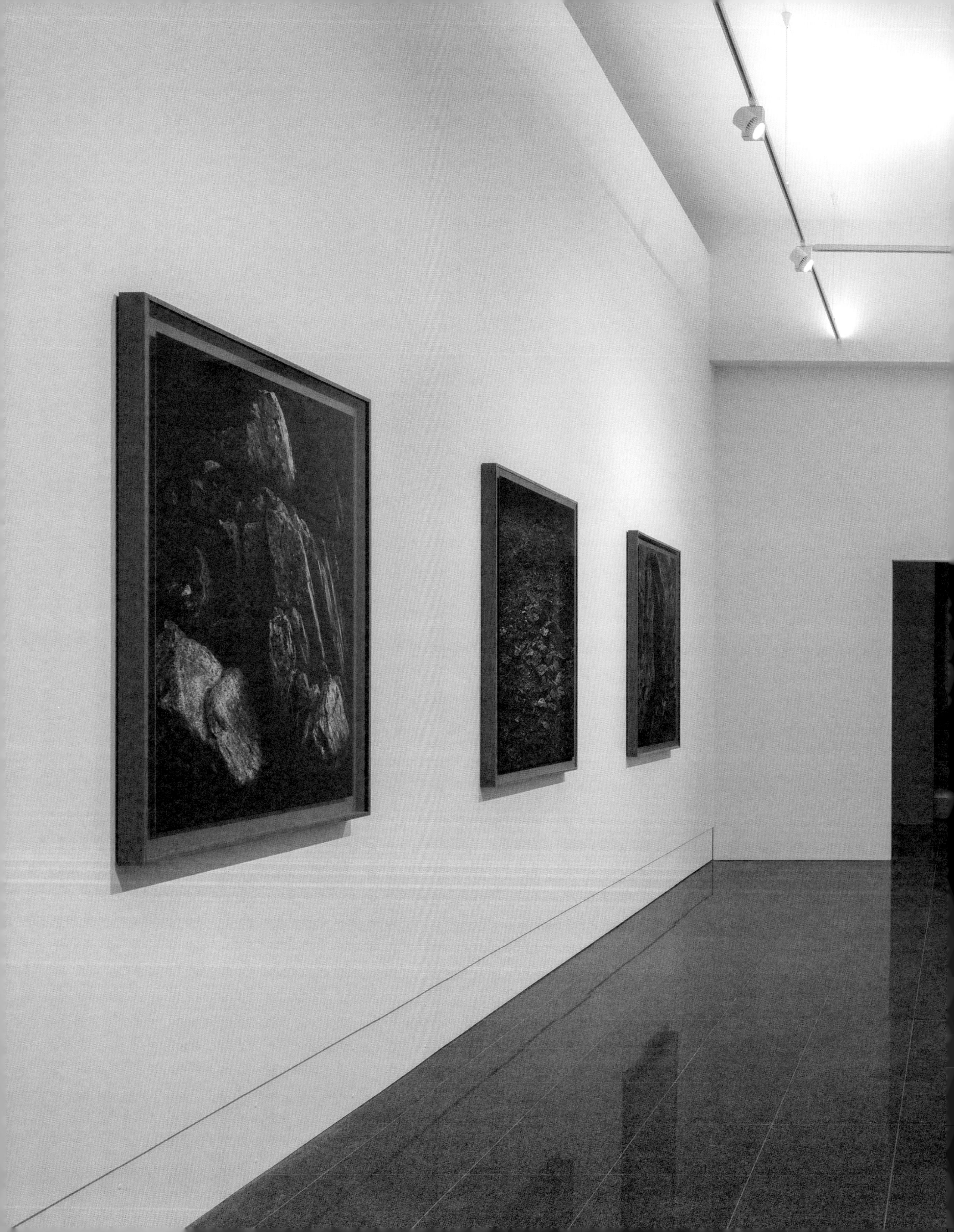

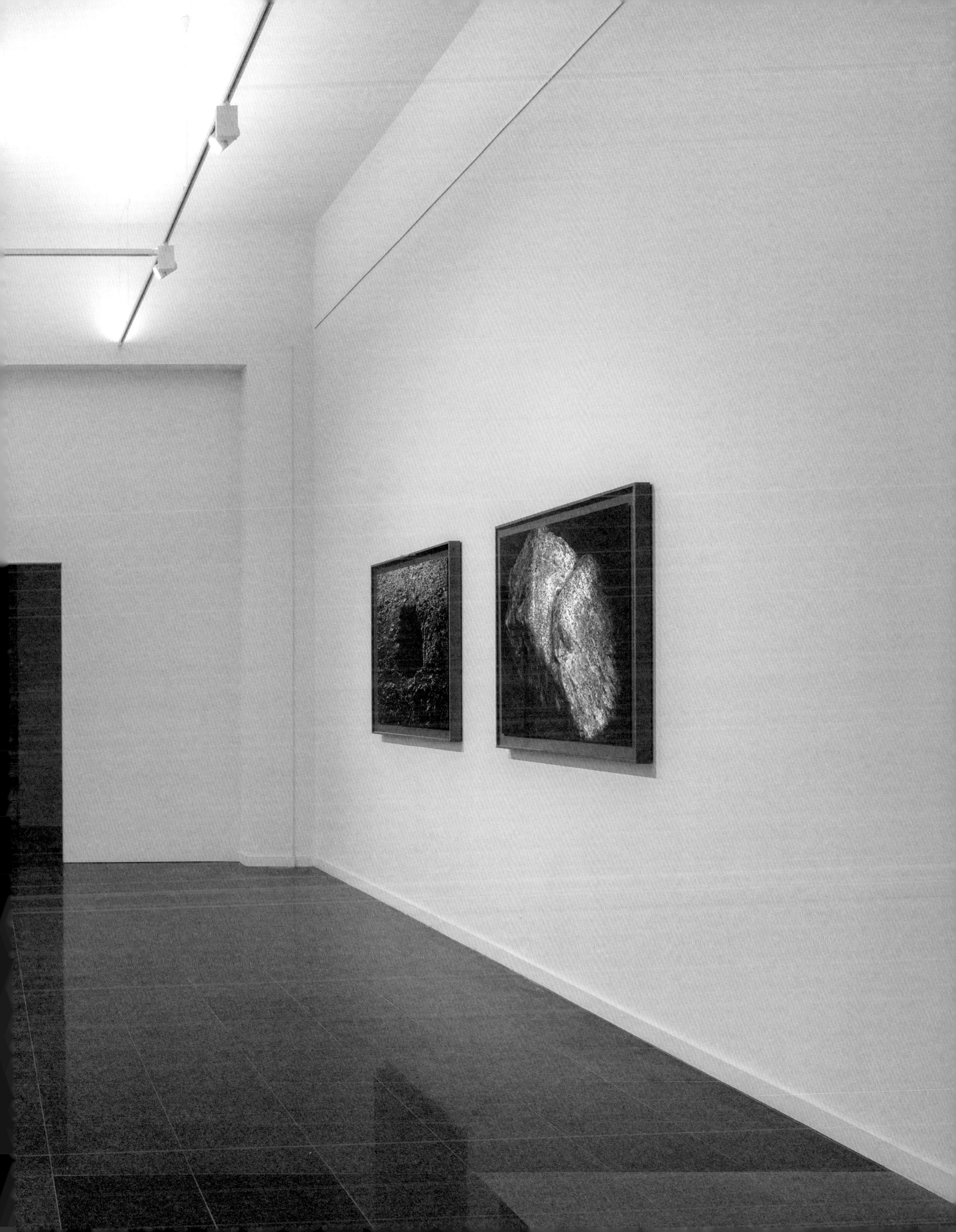

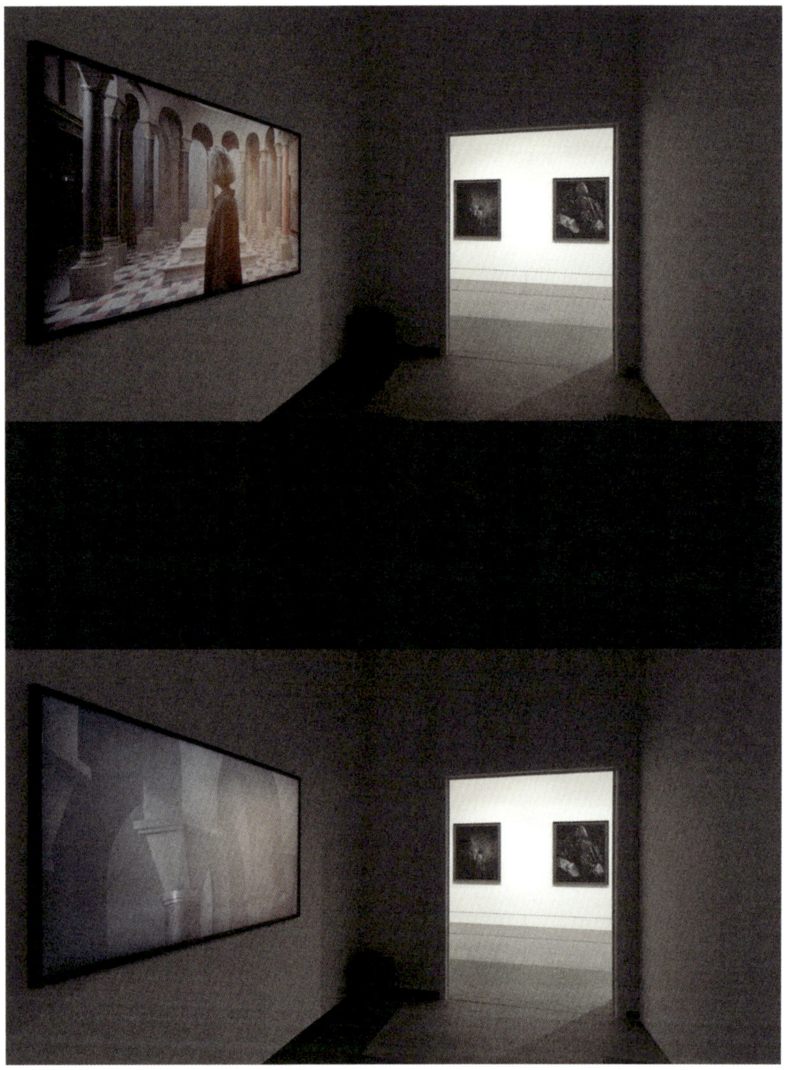

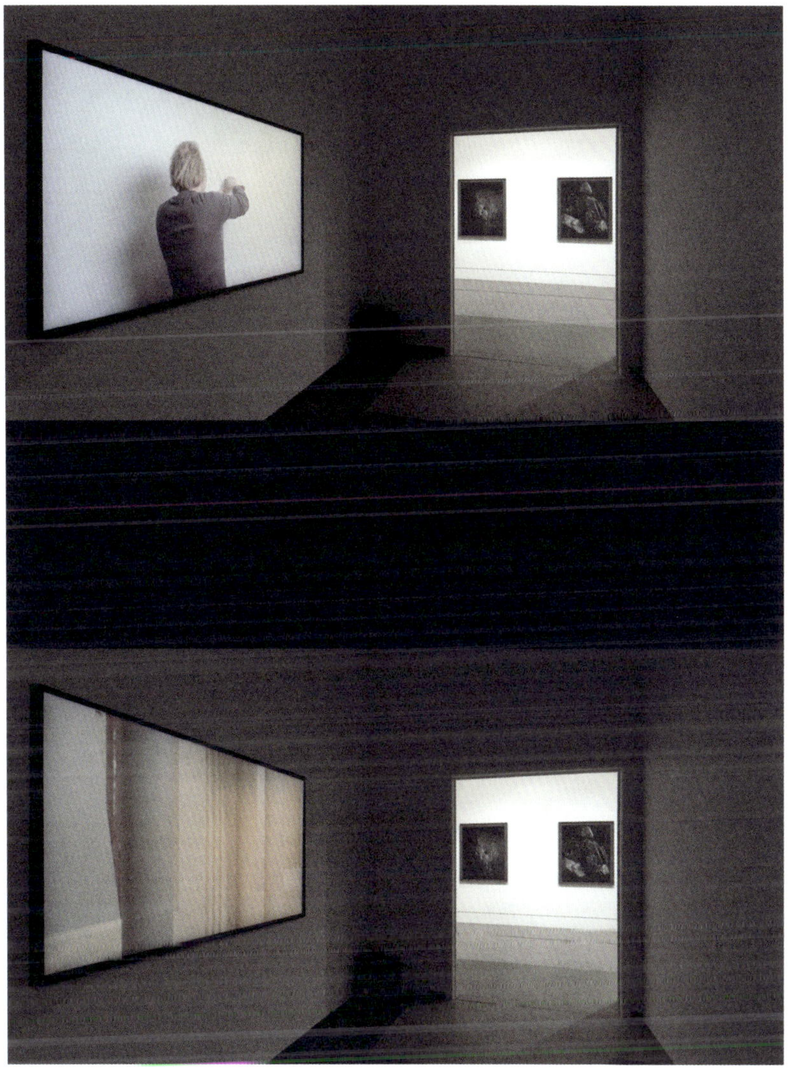

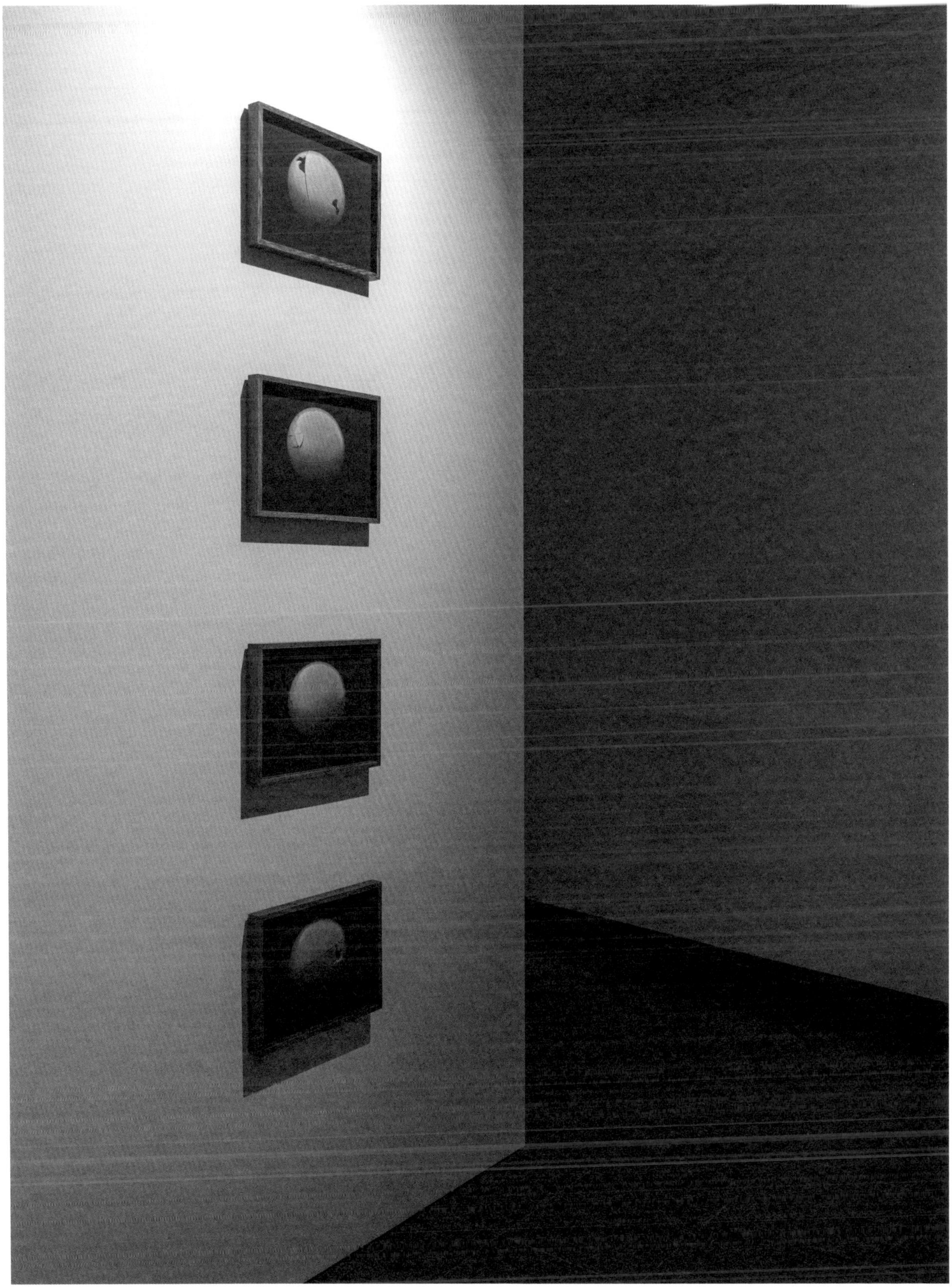

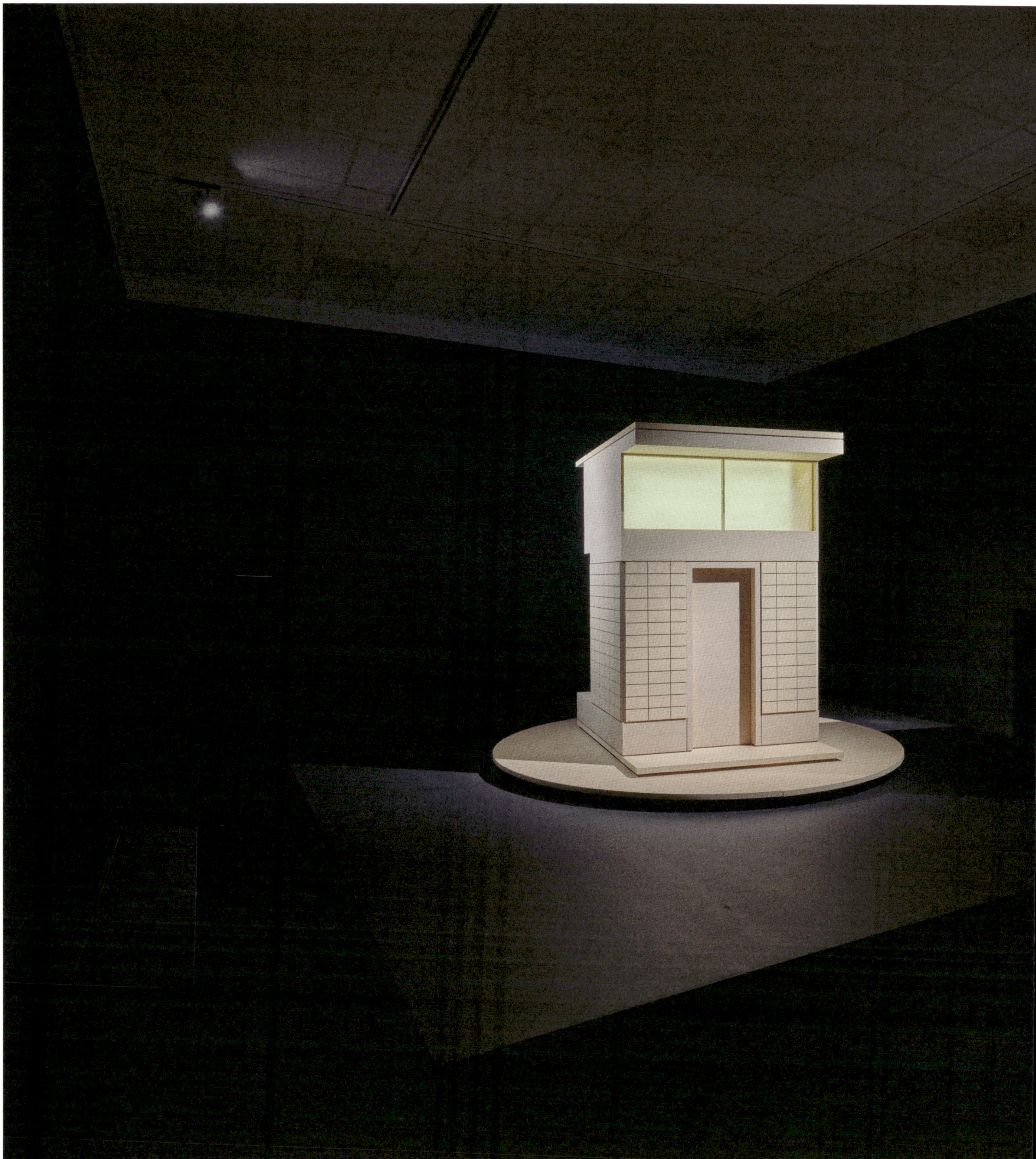

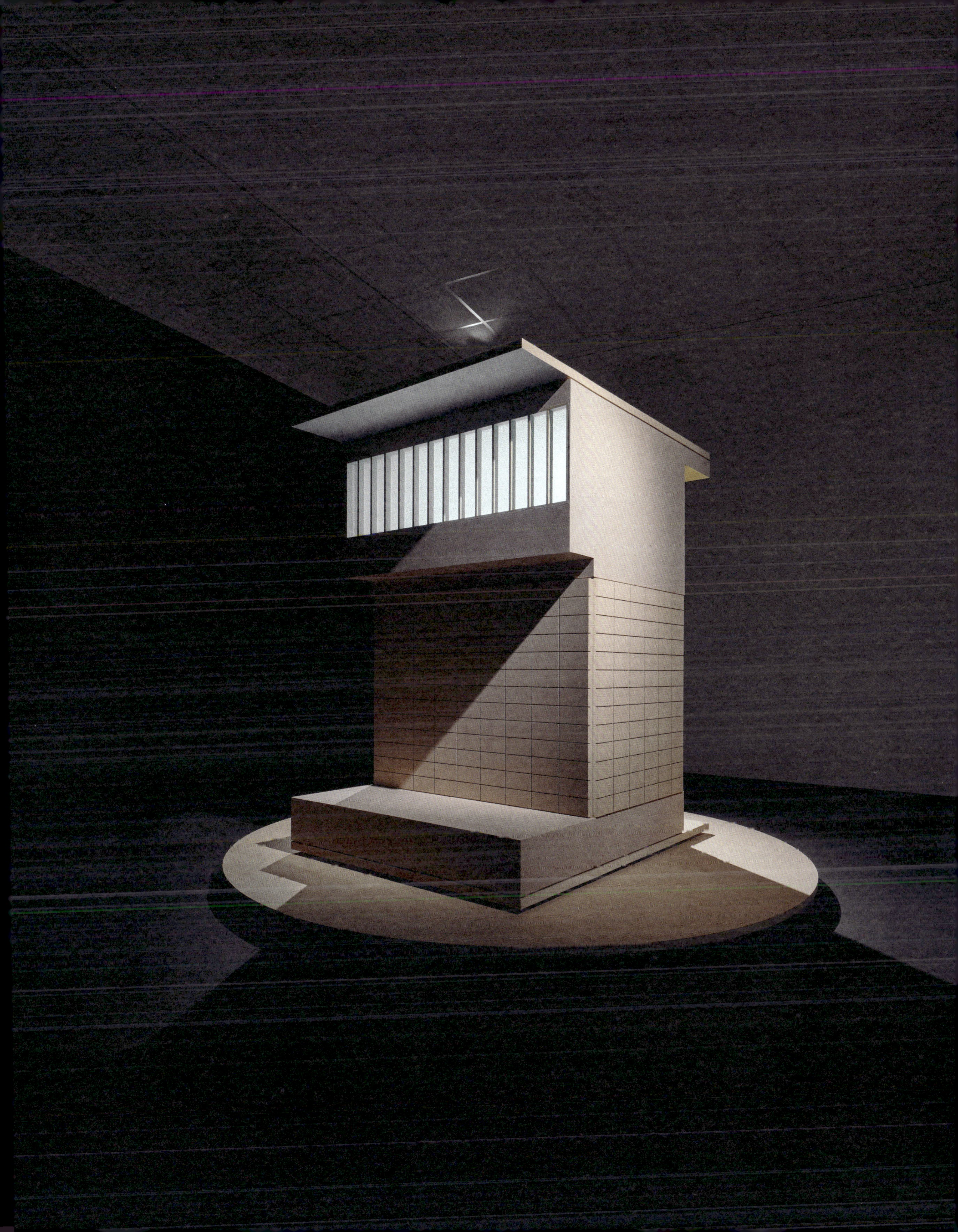

LIST OF WORKS

2014

Horizon I
870 x 1050 x 70 mm
Inkjetprint on Photorag, dibond
American walnut frame, non-reflective glass

Horizon II
870 x 1050 x 70 mm
Inkjetprint on Photorag, dibond
American walnut frame, non-reflective glass

Horizon III
870 x 1050 x 70 mm
Inkjetprint on Photorag, dibond
American walnut frame, non-reflective glass

Horizon IV
870 x 1050 x 70 mm
Inkjetprint on Photorag, dibond
American walnut frame, non-reflective glass

Horizon V
870 x 1050 x 70 mm
Inkjetprint on Photorag, dibond
American walnut frame, non-reflective glass

Horizon VI
870 x 1050 x 70 mm
Inkjetprint on Photorag, dibond
American walnut frame, non-reflective glass

Horizon VII
870 x 1050 x 70 mm
Inkjetprint on Photorag, dibond
American walnut frame, non-reflective glass

I never promised you a horizon - Model
650 x 2100 x 1950 mm
American walnut

I never promised you a horizon - Inscription
600 x 1050 x 18 mm
Medium-density fibreboard

A more elevated scene (Looking West) - Model
650 x 650 x 900 mm
Oak, medium-density fibreboard, steel

A more elevated scene (Looking West) - Horizon
870 x 1050 x 70 mm
Inkjetprint on Photorag, dibond
American walnut frame, non-reflective glass

Golden dawn (reversed)
436 x 520 x 50 mm
Inkjetprint on Photorag, dibond
American walnut frame, non-reflective glass

The promise
870 x 1050 x 70 mm
Inkjetprint on Photorag, dibond
American walnut frame, non-reflective glass

2015

La raison des ombres
1370 x 1670 x 90 mm
Inkjetprint on Photorag, dibond
American walnut frame, non-reflective glass

2016

Skull CB1
304 x 374 x 36 mm
Inkjetprint on Photorag, dibond
Wenge frame, non-reflective glass

Skull BP2
304 x 374 x 36 mm
Inkjetprint on Photorag, dibond
Wenge frame, non-reflective glass

Skull BP4
304 x 374 x 36 mm
Inkjetprint on Photorag, dibond
Wenge frame, non-reflective glass

Skull CB2
304 x 374 x 36 mm
Inkjetprint on Photorag, dibond
Wenge frame, non-reflective glass

2019

Nothing is more visible than things hidden
1370 x 1670 x 90 mm
Inkjetprint on Photorag, dibond
American walnut frame, non-reflective glass

Bonheur
1200 x 2350 x 90 mm
Inkjetprint on Photorag
American walnut frame, non-reflective glass

2020

La raison des miroirs
1470 x 1870 x 90 mm
Inkjetprint on Photorag, dibond
American walnut frame, non-reflective glass

La raison des miroirs - Reconstruction
10500 x 8700 x 5600 mm
Chipboard, medium-density fibreboard, plastics,
construction wood, acrylic paint, varnish

2021

Des ombres et miroirs I
360 x 500 x 36 mm
Inkjetprint on Photorag, dibond
Wenge frame, non-reflective glass

Des ombres et miroirs II
360 x 500 x 36 mm
Inkjetprint on Photorag, dibond
Wenge frame, non-reflective glass

Des ombres et miroirs III
360 x 500 x 36 mm
Inkjetprint on Photorag, dibond
Wenge frame, non-reflective glass

2023

Des ombres et miroirs IV
360 x 500 x 36 mm
Inkjetprint on Photorag, dibond
Wenge frame, non-reflective glass

Des ombres et miroirs V
360 x 500 x 36 mm
Inkjetprint on Photorag, dibond
Wenge frame, non-reflective glass

Des ombres et miroirs VI
360 x 500 x 36 mm
Inkjetprint on Photorag, dibond
Wenge frame, non-reflective glass

None whatsoever - Reconstruction
6500 x 4000 x 3600
Chipboard, medium-density fibreboard,
construction wood, plaster,
acrylic paint, varnish

At the break of day - Study
1200 x 1200 x 920
Medium-density fibreboard,
plastics, acrylic paint

2018-2023

Hollow
1080 x 1320 x 60 mm
Inkjetprint on Photorag, dibond
Wenge frame, non-reflective glass

Shelf
1080 x 1320 x 60 mm
Inkjetprint on Photorag, dibond
Wenge frame, non-reflective glass

Path
1080 x 1320 x 60 mm
Inkjetprint on Photorag, dibond
Wenge frame, non-reflective glass

Rock formation
1080 x 1320 x 60 mm
Inkjetprint on Photorag, dibond
Wenge frame, non-reflective glass

Rock
1080 x 1320 x 60 mm
Inkjetprint on Photorag, dibond
Wenge frame, non-reflective glass

Quarry
1080 x 1320 x 60 mm
Inkjetprint on Photorag, dibond
Wenge frame, non-reflective glass

Ash hole
1080 x 1320 x 60 mm
Inkjetprint on Photorag, dibond
Wenge frame, non-reflective glass

Fence
1080 x 1320 x 60 mm
Inkjetprint on Photorag, dibond
Wenge frame, non-reflective glass

Crossing
1080 x 1320 x 60 mm
Inkjetprint on Photorag, dibond
Wenge frame, non-reflective glass

Monolith
719 x 1460 x 60 mm
Inkjetprint on Photorag, dibond
Wenge frame, non-reflective glass

2024

At the break of day - Model
2400 x 2400 x 1840
Medium-density fibreboard, plastics,
acrylic paint, LED light